D0763921

FIELD NOTES

FIELD NOTES

A GUIDED JOURNAL FOR DOING ANTHROPOLOGY

LUIS A. VIVANCO

UNIVERSITY OF VERMONT

NEW YORK OXFORD
OXFORD UNIVERSITY PRESS

Oxford University Press is a department of the University of Oxford.
It furthers the university's objective of excellence in research,
scholarship, and education by publishing worldwide.
Oxford is a registered trademark of Oxford University Press
in the United Kingdom and certain other countries.

Published in the United States of America by
Oxford University Press
198 Madison Avenue, New York, NY 10016,
United States of America.

© 2017 by Oxford University Press

For titles covered by Section 112 of the US Higher Education
Opportunity Act, please visit www.oup.com/us/he for the
latest information about pricing and alternate formats.

All rights reserved. No part of this publication may be reproduced,
stored in a retrieval system, or transmitted, in any form or by any means,
without the prior permission in writing of Oxford University Press, or as
expressly permitted by law, by license, or under terms agreed with the
appropriate reproduction rights organization. Inquiries concerning
reproduction outside the scope of the above should be sent to the Rights
Department, Oxford University Press, at the address above.

You must not circulate this work in any other form
and you must impose this same condition on any acquirer.

Library of Congress Cataloging-in-Publication Data

Names: Vivanco, Luis Antonio, 1969– author.
Title: Field notes : a guided journal for doing anthropology / Luis A.
    Vivanco, University of Vermont.
Description: New York : Oxford University Press, [2017] | Includes
    bibliographical references.
Identifiers: LCCN 2016030159 | ISBN 9780190642198 (pbk. : alk. paper)
Subjects: LCSH: Anthropology—Fieldwork. | Ethnology—Fieldwork. |
    Anthropology—Methodology.
Classification: LCC GN34.3.F53 V58 2017 | DDC 301.072/3—dc23
    LC record available at https://lccn.loc.gov/2016030159

9 8 7 6 5 4 3 2 1
Printed by LSC Communications, Inc., United States of America

Contents

GUIDED EXERCISES

*Beginning students should prioritize "core" exercises. More advanced students should include "secondary" exercises.

CHAPTER ONE

ANTHROPOLOGY BEYOND "JUST GO DO IT"

Before heading off to conduct his first fieldwork project in 1926, renowned British social anthropologist E. E. Evans-Pritchard reportedly went to seek the advice of his professor Bronislaw Malinowski about how to actually do it. The response he got was direct, but frustratingly vague: "Don't be a bloody fool!" Coming from an advisor who claimed to have invented modern anthropological fieldwork, calling it "the ethnographer's magic," it is, perhaps, not such a surprising response. But succeeding generations of greenhorn anthropologists commonly received similarly curt and ambiguous recommendations about how to conduct fieldwork, being told such things as *Just go do it. You'll figure it out as you go. Trust your gut.*

During the past several decades, things have changed. Discussion and teaching about ethnographic fieldwork methods are no longer the "black box" they once were, and methods-related scholarly books and journal articles have proliferated. But there is a persistent sense that there are no simple recommendations, much less formal techniques, for creating and maintaining the kind of open-ended and collaborative interpersonal relationships with individuals in a community that can generate useful data in sociocultural anthropology. On some level, we anthropologists still believe that you *just have to go do it* . . . and try not to be a fool in the process!

In asking you to undertake ethnographic fieldwork, your instructor is quite possibly inspired by something similar. No one expects you to deliberately do harebrained things, nor should you. But it is likely that while conducting fieldwork, at some point—perhaps even on multiple occasions—you may *feel* like a fool. And under most circumstances of anthropological fieldwork, this feeling is not only *not* abnormal, it can actually be a *good* thing. The reason is this: one of the things that can make us feel foolish is when we do, say, or think something that seems reasonable and obvious to us, but won't to others. Taken the right way, such misunderstandings and the feelings of bewilderment, discomfort, or embarrassment that can accompany them are not signs of the futility and meaninglessness of communicating with others. Rather, they are indications that our own commonsensical notions of what is right and appropriate may not be necessarily shared universally.

To an anthropologist, such occasions are learning opportunities. Their potential is that we can move from looking through our own lens to recognizing the existence of the lens itself. More important, they help us begin to expose and decenter our own tacit and unstated assumptions enough to apprehend the tacit and unstated assumptions of others—what Malinowski famously called "the native's point of view" and American anthropologist Clifford Geertz later termed the "informal logic of everyday life." But getting at these matters—if such a thing is even possible—in the dynamic flow and messy ambiguities of actual social situations can be difficult. So it's important to learn which methods and techniques work well to elicit, record, organize, and interpret useful and relevant sociocultural data.

With the proliferation of methods-related books and articles in the past couple of decades, it has gotten a lot easier to learn about these things before actually conducting fieldwork. But conventional books about doing ethnographic fieldwork, their intended audience being graduate students, other scholars, and specialists, tend to be filled with fairly abstract descriptions and justifications of research techniques. Because they often sit on a shelf or in a filing cabinet after they've been read, these writings are also divorced from the practical process anybody actually undergoes in learning how to do these things in the real world.

This book proposes something new and different: the integration of learning, guidance, and practice into one book. Here you will learn about different dimensions and techniques of fieldwork in sociocultural anthropology by working through guided exercises—some of which you will do by yourself; some, with other people—using space in the book itself to practice and record what you are learning. This book is thus a synthesis of a basic introduction to anthropological fieldwork methods and a field note journal. The goal is to produce a stimulating and meaningful learning experience as well as a physical record of your work that will contain raw notes and reflective writings for specific class projects. It can also serve as a personal record of skill development, or a tool to help you prepare for future anthropological work. Further, because anthropological research skills are useful for anyone, another major goal of this book is to urge you on a path of developing a practical set of skills that will serve you wherever your studies, life, and career take you.

The book is divided into three parts. Although it is not an exhaustive inventory of all research techniques that fieldworkers use, each part gives practical background on and guided exercises related to key dimensions of anthropological fieldwork.

Part I: Preparing for Fieldwork

- The purpose and goals of ethnographic fieldwork
- Designing and starting a fieldwork project
- Anthropological research ethics and working with "human subjects"

Part II: Doing Fieldwork

- Developing note-taking skills
- Primary ethnographic research techniques, including observing, interviewing, mapping, and others

Part III: Working with Fieldwork Data

- Strategies for processing field notes and analyzing data
- Developing writing strategies for "thick description," evoking place, positioning yourself, and connecting stories with ideas

After introducing this theme in Part I, you will find a consistent engagement with research ethics throughout the book. Practically all aspects of doing research in human communities touch on issues of fairness, power, control, inequality, privilege, and competing purposes. This book introduces you to a number of common ethical quandaries and gives you the opportunity to reason through them in light of the discipline's ethical principles. The goal is not to offer easy resolution to the difficult issues each situation raises, but to help you develop a working knowledge of basic research ethics and the values that guide them.

You will also find various other features here to help you develop your fieldwork IQ and skillset, including "Fieldwork Tips" boxes with practical reminders and suggestions, as well as "Key Resources" boxes that identify supplemental materials chosen carefully for their usefulness and accessibility. One thing this book is *not* is a study of the origins and history of fieldwork methods in anthropology; these boxes will point you to sources on that topic. If you find the guided activities and resources helpful and want to try others, you can visit this book's companion website at www.oup.com/us/vivanco, which includes a number of additional exercises and resources.

Using This Book

This book is intended to be portable. Carry it with you when you are practicing fieldwork techniques or, beyond that, conducting actual fieldwork. Use it for jotting down observations of people doing things and what they tell you; making sketches and drawings; creating to-do lists, names of contacts, phone numbers, addresses, etc.; writing down emerging questions or ideas before you forget them; penning short descriptive vignettes; or reflecting on the experience of fieldwork itself, even venting your frustrations. Working anthropologists do all these things with their field journals.

This book is also intended to be flexible, capable of being used for a variety of individual and classroom purposes. If you are new to cultural anthropology and are enrolled in an introductory course, you may find the brief narrative background sections and exercises in Parts I and II useful as a supplement to your class readings and lectures. The division of the guided activities into "Core" and "Secondary" (see the table of "Guided Exercises") is intended to help you differentiate core foundational skills and techniques from more-specialized or more-refined practices. Completing a number of the core exercises in Parts I and II will give you a taste of fieldwork and will exist as a fine record of skill development for future work. Adding a couple of exercises in Part III will give you a sense of how anthropologists process and transform fieldwork data into a narrative, weaving together stories and ideas.

If you are enrolled in a fieldwork methods course, or a course that involves a semester-long ethnographic research project, this book could be used more intensively in all three parts, guiding you through the diverse skillsets and ethical considerations required for more-substantive projects. To your eyes, the background sections may look somewhat general and basic, especially if at the same time you are reading the methods books and journal articles mentioned before. The advantage of using this book is that you can apply the skill-building exercises here to your specific research project.

Fieldwork Skills Are Life Skills

However you use this book, the chances that you will become a professional anthropologist employing ethnographic methods in a formal research project are probably pretty slim. But you *will* use many of the perspectives and skills you work on here in your life and career beyond college, as thousands of anthropology graduates can attest. Fieldwork experience plays a special role in the formation of a toolbox of useful lifelong skills, because competency in fieldwork involves:

- **Directed learning.** By definition, fieldwork is a learning process, and fieldworkers are constantly alert to opportunities to learn something new and connect it to something they already know. Although much of this learning process is self-directed, fieldworkers need to be open to what people in their community of study think is important to learn.

- **Curiosity.** Albert Einstein once said, "It's a miracle curiosity survives modern education," because so much of formal education focuses on telling you what you should know instead of cultivating open-ended curiosity. Fieldwork requires sustained curiosity in the lives and stories of others, and fieldworkers are habitually curious.

- **Asking good questions.** A lot of scholars consider that 99% of a good answer is a good question. Fieldworkers know how to pose useful and interesting questions that can elicit meaningful responses.

- **Accuracy and attention to detail.** The credibility of a fieldworker's observations and interviews depends on documenting accurately the details of what people say and do.

- **Listening.** It has been said that one of the most sincere forms of respect is actually listening to what another has to say. Active listening is a difficult skill but lies at the heart of fieldwork.

- **Negotiation.** Building relationships with people whose lives you want to document and understand depends on the ability to reach an agreement with them about the purpose and terms of your research. This typically involves ongoing processes of give and take rooted in ethical relations with others.

- **Networking.** Fieldworkers are effective at identifying, understanding, and using social networks both to cultivate relationships and to learn about the structure of social groups.

- **Adaptability.** Fieldworkers often confront, even seek out, things that are strange to them, unexpected, and outside their normal experience. They also know that things they set out to do won't always work out: interviews get canceled, people don't show up to an appointment, and fieldworkers themselves make mistakes. And fieldwork situations are often ambiguous and loosely structured. Flexibility, adapting without judgment, and maintaining poise all are critical to dimensions of fieldwork.

- **Communication.** Being able to explain to people—especially verbally and in writing—what your research is about and why it's important requires strong communication skills, sometimes in a language other than your native tongue.

- **Recognizing, respecting, and working with difference.** One of the hallmarks of anthropology is cultural relativism, or withholding judgment about people and perspectives that seem strange or exotic. By necessity, fieldworkers develop a practical relativism based on recognition and respect for people who are different from them.

- **Critical thinking.** Fieldworkers must assess and evaluate on a regular basis the validity of their evidence. Critical reflection on what is known and still unknown can and should shape the directions of fieldwork.

I will draw your attention to these competencies as you are working through the practical exercises of this book. Now let's go do it!

PART I

PREPARING FOR FIELDWORK

One of the problems with the notion that fieldwork is something one just goes and does is that it downplays the preparation necessary to identify and create meaningful opportunities for ethnographic research. Knowledge of anthropological history and theory has long been considered a key element in that preparation, for professionals at least, because it helps them identify and frame meaningful research questions. For the beginning anthropologist who does not yet have such extensive background, however, the considerations are somewhat different. Preparing for fieldwork involves understanding, first and foremost, its goals, purposes, uses, and design principles. It is also necessary to consider the values that motivate and shape fieldwork, as well as the ethical principles that guide anthropologists in their work. The purpose of this first part of the book is to provide an overview of these matters, and to have you work through various exercises that will prepare you for the fieldwork activities that come in the second part of the book.

CHAPTER TWO

FIELDWORK

A CONCISE AND PRACTICAL OVERVIEW

Imagine yourself suddenly set down, alone outside the gated edge of a large, partially walled urban estate. As you stroll through the gates, you are struck by the carefully tended grassy meadows, old buildings encased in creeping vines, and the air of serious purposefulness among the people moving around this place. You proceed to a quadrangle surrounded by old buildings and enter one of them. Wandering its wood-paneled halls, you realize the individual chambers here are empty of people. Deeper into the sanctum, you encounter another chamber, large and arena-like, where the occupants of this building appear to have assembled. Nobody notices as you silently file in the back, and in front of you sits an attentive crowd facing a young adult, a novice by the looks of it, who is holding forth in oration. Eventually the novice quiets and older individuals in the assembly begin making orations of their own, to which the novice responds. It is clear from their self-assuredness that these individuals are authorities in the specialized ritual language that the novice was speaking. While most of the words being spoken here are obscure to you, one word draws your attention because it is often uttered with reverence. That word is *fieldwork*. You realize now that you've read about this before—it's a rite of passage called a "fieldwork proposal defense." This is a university campus, these people are anthropologists, and they are gathered to evaluate an advanced student's readiness to go to the mysterious and sacred place of discovery and trials known as "the Field"...

The Goals, Purposes, and Uses of Fieldwork

Chances are you will never endure this rite of passage, a common one for graduate students in cultural anthropology just before they begin their thesis research. But as cheeky as the vignette above may read, **fieldwork**—participant observation in a community to investigate its behaviors and beliefs—does carry potent significance for anthropologists, such that C.G. Seligman, Malinowski's own teacher, once told him that fieldwork is to anthropology what the blood of the martyrs is to the church (McGee and Warms 2013: 762). In anthropology, fieldwork is more than a collection of techniques for generating and accumulating data. For many, doing fieldwork is, quite simply, *doing anthropology*. It is a core practice that integrates the primary philosophical elements of the discipline—especially culture, holism, and relativism—into a single frame of inquiry. It is also tied to the creation of an identity: experience and success in it, as well as where it is performed, define one's membership and expertise in the anthropological community. When anthropologists refer to fieldwork they often assume these intertwined intellectual, experiential, and identity-shaping elements (Robben and Sluka 2012).

Although cultural anthropologists use and produce quantitative data for certain projects, fieldwork is a form of **qualitative research**, an investigative approach whose goal is to produce in-depth and detailed descriptions and analyses of variables in the setting in which they occur naturally. Qualitative fieldwork is defined by these primary attributes (modified and adapted from Robben and Sluka 2012):

- **Humanism.** Humanism places fundamental value on human experience, meaning, creativity, and morality. Understanding these things involves acts of interpretation and translation.
- **Scientific empiricism.** Empiricism is at the heart of the scientific method, representing a commitment to produce evidence through observation, description, documentation, and experimentation. Anthropological fieldwork involves all of these except experimentation.

KEY RESOURCE. "Imagine yourself suddenly set down . . ." I didn't invent that; it is the famous expression that opens Bronislaw Malinowski's *Argonauts of the Western Pacific*, the 1922 book that laid out the aims and scope of ethnographic fieldwork. Check out his first chapter, which is still widely read (Malinowski 1922).

KEY RESOURCE. Antonius Robben and Jeffrey Sluka's book *Ethnographic Fieldwork: An Anthropological Reader* (Robben and Sluka 2012) is an excellent compendium of original writings from throughout the history of the discipline, examining diverse aspects of fieldwork.

- **Particularism and case study.** An approach that studies a particular group of people, events, and institutions over time, going deep into the details of the case. It involves a commitment to the close-up and microscale and is typically based on long-term involvement in a community that goes well beyond a short visit or survey.

- **Cross-cultural perspective.** A comparative approach that considers specifics about human behavior or thought, with an awareness that people in other places, times, and social positions might behave or think differently. It is tied closely to cultural relativism and recognizes the existence of multiple truths, but it also supports generalization because it allows comparison.

- **Holism.** Fieldworkers strive to understand the systematic interconnections among beliefs, practices, and social institutions across multiple domains of a society (kinship, politics, economics, religion, etc.).

- **Prolonged experiential immersion.** Intimate personal experience through immersion in other people's routines of everyday life produces important knowledge and is the "participant" side in participant observation. The fieldworker personally is the instrument of research and data generation, learning about the meaning people give to their lives through direct experiential involvement in a cross section of their everyday activities.

- **Planned, yet eclectic.** Fieldwork is intentional and framed by research questions and objectives. But social situations are often ambiguous and fluid, and fieldwork is eclectic and improvisational as the fieldworker responds flexibly to circumstances, opportunities, and serendipity to learn new things. Fieldworkers are open to not always knowing where the project is headed.

- **Methods as repertoire.** Fieldwork is not a set of technical procedures or formulas but instead a "repertoire," or range of skills and techniques a researcher draws on, and even contrives, depending on the context.

- **Reflexivity.** Critical self-reflection ("reflexivity") on how the researcher's own biases, privileges, personal histories, and perceptions shape the interpretations and points of view he or she develops about the subject.

- **Collaboration and trust.** Establishing and maintaining mutually beneficial and trusting interpersonal relationships is a key condition of fieldwork. Participants in the research are collaborators whose needs and concerns should be equal to the fieldworker's.

Fieldwork is a method that prioritizes deep, long, and slow involvement. It is not appropriate for all social-research projects. But working together, these attributes can provide a powerful means of learning new things about people's lives, including the fieldworker's own life.

You probably noticed that some of these attributes exist in tension with or opposition to the others. It is perhaps one reason why it is often said that fieldwork is simultaneously art and science, bridging humanistic and scientific styles of inquiry.

FIELDWORK TIP

Fieldwork is especially useful for:

- defining a problem when it's not yet clear what the problem is
- understanding problems that have no single explanation or solution
- exploring complex, multifaceted systems and relationships
- identifying and clarifying connections between social phenomena when those connections are not well understood
- identifying the basic assumptions people make about something, and how those assumptions connect (or don't connect) to behavior
- identifying who is affected by a social problem or conflict
- documenting a social process
- clarifying why a program has failed
- identifying unexpected outcomes and unintended consequences
- complementing or complicating quantitative data

(list adapted from LeCompte and Schensul 1999)

| **2.1** | **Fieldwork's Attributes: A Practical Appraisal** |

Reviewing the list above, which of fieldwork's attributes would you identify as "art" and which ones as "science?"

CRITICAL THINKING • COMMUNICATION

ART   SCIENCE

_____   _____

_____   _____

_____   _____

_____   _____

Now, reviewing the list again, identify more-specific oppositions and commonalities between any of these attributes. Jot down at least two of each here and briefly note how and why they are opposed or complementary.

Oppositions:

_____

_____

_____

Complementarities:

_____

_____

_____

The goal of fieldwork is typically *not* to produce results that are testable and replicable by other researchers, such as it is with the classic scientific method (figure 2.1). Rather, its goal is to produce a *trustworthy account* of a group of people, a social process, an event, or an institution. There are three primary reasons for this key difference:

1. *Replication is impractical* because it is usually impossible for two or more fieldworkers to describe a social setting in exactly the same way. Social settings are dynamic and multifaceted, and so fieldworkers may confront different empirical realities, especially if time has passed between their periods of fieldwork. More important,

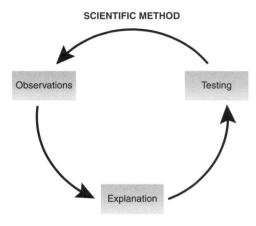

FIGURE 2.1   The classic scientific method is circular. If you had to visualize the ethnographic method, how would it look? Draw it to the side.

fieldworkers have differences in background, personality, social identity, theoretical inclination, and perception that shape and filter their observations, how others will interact with them, and how they will interpret the significance of their observations and experiences. Having said that, fieldwork can be conducted by teams, and the team often spends a lot of time evaluating and aligning different observations and assumptions made by team members.

2. *Fieldwork is not experimental*; that is, it does not perform tests, utilize control groups, or use deductive reasoning in an attempt to falsify a hypothesis. Instead, like other forms of qualitative research, it employs **inductive reasoning**, which works with specific observations and looks for patterns in them in order to develop generalizations and insights. In this process, *contextualization* replaces falsification, and hypotheses—if they play a role in fieldwork at all—are educated hunches about what might be going on.

3. *Fieldworkers are not gathering objective data* in any simple and straightforward sense. As Johannes Fabian (Fabian 1971) once observed, fieldwork is not like "collecting blackberries." Ethnographic facts are not simply sitting around, waiting to be picked up or discovered. Fieldworkers make observations and ask members of the community about what they have been seeing and hearing, which typically elicits various explanations and interpretations. Fieldworkers actively select and synthesize with those individuals what actual details will become data, in a process that Fabian recognized was neither objective nor subjective, but **intersubjective**, which refers to the joint creation of comprehension and meaning

FIELDWORK TIP

Beyond "Informants"? The term "informant" doesn't necessarily capture the complexity of the relationship between fieldworkers and the individuals with whom they work. It also has a vaguely furtive and legalistic connotation (as in "police informant"). So it is worth it to give thought to alternatives. Some anthropologists use the term "collaborators" (evoking a shared enterprise), others use "interlocutor" (evoking ongoing conversations), and still others use "consultants" (evoking advice shared by experts)—or all of these (and more) depending on the kind of relationship. Can you think of another term that might work, and what kind of relationship it would suggest?

between a fieldworker and the subjects of his or her research. This relationship of collaboration is more subtle than the traditional word for a fieldworker's subjects—"informant"—because collaborators in the research are not simply "providing information" to the fieldworker.

These points raise an immediate (and justified) question: How do we know if the fieldwork was dismally performed, or worse, just made up out of the fieldworker's fertile imagination? In other words, how do we actually know if an ethnographic account is *trustworthy*? Judging fieldwork as reliable, valid, and rigorous is based on how the work addresses several questions (Shenton 2004):

- Is it ***credible***? Is there evidence that the fieldworker had prolonged engagement in the community, used a variety of methods, and followed ethical principles?
- *Is it **plausible**?* Does it create an empirical account that is believable? Can that empirical account be reasonably subjected to reinterpretation?
- *Is it **transferable**?* Is there enough detail in the findings to be able to apply insights to a different setting?
- *Is it **dependable**?* Is there consistency between the evidence presented and the claims or conclusions made? Is there an explanation of how data were generated? Is the description clear?
- *Is it **confirmable**?* Is there evidence that the findings were confirmed with informants and reliable scholars, scholarship, or both?

These questions are asked at all stages of research—when planning a fieldwork project, during fieldwork itself when reflecting critically on the process and findings, and especially when communicating fieldwork data and findings, such as in an academic conference, journal publication, or even blog post.

In spite of these differences in goals and standards of validity, one thing all social, natural, and physical scientists do share in common is curiosity about the empirical world, an alert and inquisitive bearing based on the desire to explore, investigate, and learn new things. In anthropology, cultivating the habitual curiosity required for successful fieldwork is supported by the development of certain skills, knowing how to ask good questions being one of them (see chapter 7). But it also begins by assessing what you most want to learn about people's lives.

DIRECTED LEARNING • CURIOSITY • ASKING GOOD QUESTIONS

2.2   Cultivating Curiosity

Anthropology attracts curious people. Think of a curious person you know; what are the primary qualities of that curious person? What factors might prevent someone from being curious?

_____

_____

_____

Curiosity drives anthropological inquiry. Make a list here of at least **five** issues or themes about *anything* having to do with humans and their lives that you are *really* curious about. Next to each, write one sentence about *why* you're curious about it.

1. _____

2. _____

3. _____

4. _____

5. _____

Connecting curiosity to fieldwork: In what *two* social settings, communities, or groups—*anywhere* in the world—do you think you could explore each of those themes?

_____

_____

_____

_____

_____

_____

_____

_____

_____

_____

Locating "the Field"

Anthropological fieldwork does not require anybody to go off and live among a group of people on a remote coral atoll, tropical jungle settlement, or desert camp. It certainly can—and for a long time, that kind of thing was expected—but the older view of what anthropologists do was rooted in the idea that it is necessary to "set off for the field"; that is, make a physical and social break from home to immerse themselves, with singular purpose, in the face-to-face relationships of a culturally different group of people (Amit 2000, Vivanco 2013). This idea imagines "the field" as a geographically distant, isolated—even exotic—place to be discovered.

For a number of reasons, anthropologists have moved beyond this narrow view of the field. One reason is that there simply aren't people out there, isolated and waiting to "be discovered," thanks to ongoing histories of globalization that touch people's lives in complex ways. Moreover, the act of "discovering" people does not carry the aura of virtue it once did, which during the era of European colonization meant bringing those "newly discovered" peoples (for Europeans, at least) into a sphere of Western influence and power, with many destructive social impacts. People are also on the move—transients, migrants, nomads, refugees, cosmopolitans, and others whose lives can spread across nations and regions—eroding the obligatory notion of fieldwork as a practice involving dwelling in a single, far-off place. And of course, there are anthropologically interesting social settings that simply don't correspond to a physical territory or entail face-to-face interactions, including virtual worlds such as World of Warcraft or Internet platforms such as Facebook or Twitter.

KEY RESOURCE. The essay "Writing against Culture" by Lila Abu-Lughod (Abu-Lughod 1991) explores the dilemmas of feminist, native, and "halfie" anthropologists—those with one foot in academic anthropology and the other in their own culture, which unsettles boundaries between self and other and can produce a "split self."

Perhaps the strongest reason, though, is that anthropological fieldwork now takes place in every imaginable situation where there are people who are doing things and interacting with each other, which naturally includes our own home communities. Indeed, many anthropologists (such as myself) who have worked for long periods in geographically distant communities—the "classic" settings of anthropological fieldwork—have also conducted research "at home." Fieldwork settings at home can be as ambiguous and fluid as anywhere else, but the actual work may be episodic as we balance short bursts of fieldwork with our more-normal duties and roles; the line between our identities as "natives" blurs with our role as fieldworkers, and the participants in our research include, in addition to strangers new to us, friends and neighbors who we know much better (Vivanco 2013).

These details each can present certain challenges, but the broader point here is that what defines anthropological fieldwork is not really the act of separating from our everyday lives to immerse ourselves continuously in intensive social life elsewhere. Rather, it is the deliberate work of identifying, creating, and cultivating relationships and interactions that yield meaningful insights into other people's lives, without assuming that we as fieldworkers stand apart from or outside them (Amit 2000, Vivanco 2013). These things can happen anywhere and in pretty much any social context.

2.3   The Field in Your Backyard

DIRECTED LEARNING • CURIOSITY

In your own "backyard" (hometown, campus community, or city where you live), there are countless opportunities for anthropological fieldwork. Each of the categories below represents a type of fieldwork context for you to consider. Next to each category, write at least *two* concrete examples from your own "backyard" in which you could imagine yourself doing fieldwork:

Event (festival, celebration, ritual, meeting, etc.):

Journey (pilgrimage, trip on a bus, weekend trip, etc.):

Transaction (buying and selling a good or service, exchange of objects, etc.):

Social institution (hospital clinic, government office, etc.):

Association or interest group (club, religious community, etc.):

Conflict (dispute over a public good, interpersonal squabble, etc.):

Social process (planning a dog park, organizing a social protest, filing a court case, etc.):

Public space (train station, park, cafeteria, etc.):

Explain which of these eight categories most interests you and why.

_____

_____

_____

_____

Making the Familiar Strange . . .

One of the dilemmas of backyard anthropology is that, like the fish that doesn't see the water it swims in, we don't always recognize culturally salient and meaningful dynamics because we often make the same unstated assumptions as the people whose lives we are investigating. Doing fieldwork anywhere can be aided by cultivating a "beginner's mind," an attitude of openness and a willingness to check one's preconceptions, but these qualities are especially important in one's own backyard, where so much seems familiar and obvious. Yet there is no easy prescription for achieving these things. Many anthropologists believe a primary strategy involves what John Comaroff (Comaroff 2010: 530) calls **critical estrangement**—that is, taking the familiar and taken for granted and making it seem strange, "deconstructing its surfaces and . . . relativizing . . . its horizons." As Comaroff observes, anthropologists are always asking:

> *"What is it that actually gives substance to the dominant discourses and conventional practices of that world, to its subject positions and*

Hortense Powdermaker (1896–1970) was a well-known American anthropologist who observed, "Anthropology is a profession in which it is an asset for the practitioners to be somewhat outside of their own society and of the ones they study, and yet be able to step into them and relate to people. Certain personality types carry this dual role of involvement and detachment more easily than do others and even enjoy it" (Powdermaker 1966: 303).

its semiosis, its received categories and their unruly undersides, to the manner in which it is perceived and experienced, fabricated, and contested?"

In other words, critical estrangement involves inquiring into the sociocultural conditions and unstated assumptions that give rise to and help sustain a particular way of thinking and acting, and appreciating how "natives" perceive and experience those things.

You should recognize the tension here. Fieldwork values intimacy and knowledge gained from firsthand experience, yet making things strange involves taking an objectifying step back, or to the side, to appreciate what's going on just under the surface. It's an old (and ongoing) debate whether one should strive to balance these tensions or emphasize one over the other. But one way to work with this issue is to deliberately play with perspective, recognizing how each perspective generates certain kinds of opportunities and dilemmas, advantages and disadvantages.

2.4 Insider/Outsider Accounts

Take an everyday thing you do (eat a meal or tie your shoes, for example) and (1) write 250 words describing each step in the process from your personal perspective, and then (2) write 250 words about it in an intentionally distancing "objective" mode, as if you were observing yourself doing it from afar (as, for example, the walk through a college campus that opens this section). Write these accounts on a computer and print them up. Use the space here to reflect on these questions.

Which of these reads "better" to you? Why? List the advantages and disadvantages of each account.

_____

_____

_____

_____
_____
_____
_____
_____
_____
_____
_____
_____
_____

KEY RESOURCE: THE NACIREMA ISSUE. After conducting this exercise, you might want to read Horace Miner's 1956 classic "Body Ritual among the Nacirema"—a piece satirizing the objectifying tendencies of anthropologists, as well as the challenges of representing one's own culture—and reflect on (1) what his point is, and (2) what he thinks the real purpose of fieldwork on one's own culture should be.

Another side to this issue is recognizing that you, as the instrument of research yourself, carry certain qualities as an individual—some within your control and others not—that shape what and how you see things, as well as how others see you in ways that affect their willingness to make space and time for you in their lives. Some qualities might be generally useful for creating certain kinds of relationships—for example, being a college student can, in theory at least, make it easier to meet and integrate yourself in the lives of other college students. But in other circumstances, some qualities can inhibit you, especially qualities you may be less aware of, including your implicit social privileges or biases others carry about you.

2.5   Unpacking Your "Invisible Knapsack"

NEGOTIATION

Recognizing your implicit social privileges and the tacit biases that others carry about you are critical dimensions of reflexive fieldwork. The idea of an "invisible knapsack" comes from Peggy McIntosh (McIntosh 1997), who focuses on white privilege. As she says, the privilege that comes with having light-colored skin is "like an invisible weightless knapsack of special provisions, assurances, tools, maps, guides, code-books, passports, visas, clothes, compass, emergency gear, and blank checks" that allows whites a range of social action and acceptance not accorded to those with darker skin. Skin color is just one factor that can open some doors and close others in fieldwork. What implicit privileges do you carry that might affect how other individuals interact with you? What tacit biases might people you interact with have about you? Try to come up with *at least four* on each side and list them here. Be as specific as you can be (for example, "being a man" isn't precise enough; something such as "as a male I can walk through campus at night without fear of sexual harassment" is the level of specificity you should be going for).

Your PRIVILEGES   **BIASES others may carry about you**

_____

_____

_____

Choose one privilege and one bias. How do you think you might limit or manage their impact on your fieldwork?

_____

_____

_____

_____

_____

_____

_____

_____

_____

_____

_____

_____

• RECOGNIZING AND WORKING WITH DIFFERENCE • CRITICAL THINKING

> **KEY RESOURCE.** The advice here on designing a fieldwork project is adapted from Margaret LeCompte and Jean Schensul's *Designing and Conducting Ethnographic Research* (LeCompte and Schensul 1999). For more-detailed perspectives on research design, see their chapter 4.

Planning and Designing a Fieldwork Project

Given the fluidity and deliberate eclecticism of fieldwork, a fieldworker can lose focus. This is one reason a fieldwork project is planned ahead of time. The objective of the planning process is to create a flexible research design that takes into consideration a number of concerns:

- **Analytical concerns**. What questions motivate the research? What are the characteristics of the fieldwork context, and how and why are they appropriate for addressing those questions? Is there a basic conceptual starting point, or theoretical approach, for this project? What are the primary approaches to data collection?
- **Resource concerns**. What resources are necessary to conduct the project, such as time, funding for travel and living expenses, or help from trained assistants? What are the grants or other forms of funding available to support the project?
- **Logistical/methodological concerns**. Has the appropriate fieldwork setting been identified? Has permission or access to key gatekeepers, sponsors, or stakeholders in them been granted? What is the timeline for the project? Who will the participants in the project be, and what guidelines will be used to select them?
- **Power/ethical concerns**. Who will benefit from—or be negatively affected by—the research? Whose interests will be served by the research? Who will own the research? What is the plan to protect the confidentiality of the participants in the research?
- **Fieldworker positionality concerns**. How will the fieldworker's national, gender, racial, sexual, and/or ethnic identities shape the his or her social position, fieldwork process, and the other concerns listed here?

Answers to these questions are typically expressed in a research proposal, but depending on to whom the proposal is addressed—the typical audiences being a research funding agency, a university human subjects review committee (see chapter 3), or a committee of professors approving a fieldwork project—the issues addressed can vary.

| 2.6 | Planning a Fieldwork Project—A Basic Worksheet |

As you develop your idea for a research project or begin your class assignment, use this worksheet to jot down answers to the following questions. This should be a living document—revise it as you work through later sections of this book, and as your ideas, interests, and questions evolve and shift.

PART 1: THE BIG QUESTIONS

What do you want to know? Fill in the blanks:

I am studying _____

Because I want to find out _____

In order to understand _____

What research questions do you have?

_____

_____

_____

What techniques do you plan to use?

_____

_____

_____

PART 2: THE FIELDWORK CONTEXT

What is the fieldwork context you plan to research?

_____

_____

_____

Where can you go for basic information about the fieldwork context?

_____

_____

_____

DIRECTED LEARNING • CURIOSITY • ASKING GOOD QUESTIONS • ACCURACY AND ATTENTION TO DETAIL • NETWORKING

What initial steps do you think you should take to start your field project?

_____

_____

_____

How will you gain access to the community you want to study?

_____

_____

_____

Who are the gatekeepers, sponsors, or stakeholders you need to know?

_____

_____

_____

How might aspects of your own identity shape your social position and the fieldwork process?

_____

_____

_____

What do you anticipate will be difficult about this project?

_____

_____

_____

PART 3: RESOURCES, LOGISTICS, AND METHODS

Who will you observe? / Who will the participants and collaborators in the research be?

_____

_____

_____

What is your timeline?

_____

_____

_____

Do you need any special equipment?

_____

_____

_____

PART 4: POWER RELATIONS AND ETHICS

Who will control the findings?

_____

_____

_____

Whose interests will it serve?

_____

_____

_____

Who benefits from the research?

_____

_____

_____

A Final Word . . . on Stuff

There is much to be said for traveling light, and in general, ethnographic fieldwork enables it since it doesn't require much stuff. Fieldworkers typically carry small unobtrusive notebooks or writing pads and a reliable writing utensil, with a few extras on hand for when the ink runs dry or the pencil lead breaks. There's a lot of room for personal preference, but reliability counts—you want this stuff to perform when you need it. A camera for taking still shots and video as well as a digital voice recorder can also be useful equipment, if you don't have a smartphone that does these things. Most anthropologists also use some kind of device—such as a laptop computer, tablet, or smartphone—for typing up field notes. And that's kind of it, unless there is some more specialized technical concern such as mapmaking. As you work through this book, I'll draw your attention to any special equipment needs and the conditions under which you might want to use certain devices—or *not* use them, as the case may be, since introducing notepads, smartphones, and so on can disrupt your interactions with others.

Space for Extra Notes

CHAPTER THREE

FIELDWORK VALUES AND ETHICS

One of the central premises of research in the natural and social sciences is that gathering data and codifying knowledge are value-neutral activities. For a number of reasons, this view has come under critical scrutiny, starting with revelations after World War II of deadly Nazi experiments on concentration camp internees, and the withholding of medical treatment from African Americans in the Tuskegee Syphilis Experiment (1932–1972) by the US government. One consequence of these revelations is that since the 1970s, research involving people—"human subjects" in bureaucratic parlance—typically has to show that protections are in place to ensure that the research causes no harm, a requirement that extends to social-scientific fields such as anthropology. But even with protections in place, researchers are not entirely free from value judgments in their work, since these judgments are foundational to the work itself. Consider the idea that research involves a search for reality or truth. From a cross-cultural perspective, the notion that there is one reality or truth, discoverable through human reason and empiricism, is a value judgment.

KEY RESOURCE. A useful overview of the events and institutional dynamics that led to the creation of human-subjects protections is covered in Carolyn Fluehr-Lobban's book *Ethics and the Profession of Anthropology* (Fluehr-Lobban 2003).

More than any other social-scientific discipline, anthropology is open to recognizing this issue; for example, through cultural relativism. But the discipline's associations with 19th- and 20th-century colonialism and the extension of state power over indigenous, minority, and poor communities have produced distrust and suspicion in some quarters about the implicit values shaping anthropological research. The distrust continues, some critics assert, when researchers fail to recognize how their work is *not* a value-neutral enterprise, such as when it oversimplifies another culture's lifeways through labeling and classification, which can reinforce stereotyping, when it gets used by powerful institutions or interests to disempower the vulnerable, or when it reinforces the authority of the anthropologist's voice over local voices (Tuhiwai Smith 2012). An alternative set of values is rooted in approaching people as "collaborators" and not as "subjects":

- **Openness**, about the intentions and outcomes of the research;

- **Ongoing negotiation**, over what is included in the study and who will control the data it creates;

- **Nonessentialism**, or avoiding oversimplifying people's lives by taking care not to reproduce stereotypes about them.

While all fieldwork involves the creation of trusting relationships, not all fieldworkers embrace these particular values in equal measure. For example, these values are more common among fieldworkers who work with vulnerable and socially marginal communities. Other contexts, such as studying how a social elite or powerful group maintains a pattern of widespread social inequality, may not involve a similarly collaborative approach.

3.1   Identifying Fieldwork's Values

CRITICAL THINKING • COMMUNICATION

When we talk about "values," we are referring to the relative preferences about how to do something in an appropriate fashion, and what its outcome should be. It is the territory of "how things ought to be." Being reflexive about fieldwork requires understanding that it carries values, what those values are, and how they might carry certain kinds of consequences for the fieldworker and individuals who participate in the fieldwork—as well as what alternative values might look like. Make a list here of values you can identify in fieldwork. Start with three or four, but add to it as you work through the exercises in this book.

_____

_____

_____

How do you think these values compare and contrast with another discipline you are studying?

_____

_____

_____

_____

_____

_____

_____

When we get into "how things ought to be," we are also dealing with **ethics**, moral questions about right and wrong and appropriate standards of behavior. Ethics in anthropology—the moral principles that guide anthropological conduct—are not just a list of do's and don't's; but are deeply connected to what it means to be a good anthropologist (Fluehr-Lobban 2003). The reason is that as fieldworkers we cannot divorce ourselves and our own actions from the communities in which we work, and we must be aware of and take responsibility for the actual and potential consequences our work has for collaborators, the community, ourselves, and for the profession as a whole.

Anthropologists are pioneers in publicly articulating our professional ethical principles. As early as the 1940s, applied anthropologists produced a code of ethics (one of the very first produced by a professional organization), and in the early 1970s the discipline as a whole followed suit through the primary national organization, the American Anthropological Association (AAA). The principles have been revised over time, responding to changes inside and outside the discipline. Since 2012, the AAA's Principles of Professional Responsibility state:

- Do no harm
- Be open and honest regarding your own work
- Obtain informed consent and necessary permissions

In their classic book *Ethnography: Principles in Practice*, Martyn Hammersley and Paul Atkinson observed, "We cannot escape the social world which we study; we are part of it. This is not a matter of methodological commitment, it is an existential fact" (Hammersley and Atkinson 1983: 15).

- Weigh competing obligations due collaborators and affected parties
- Make your results accessible
- Protect and preserve your records
- Maintain respectful and ethical professional relationships

They are not "rules" for a reason: rules are inflexible, compelling you to do what someone else thinks to be right. Not following the rules leads to threat or punishment. Instead, they are called "principles" because they are meant to provide guidance for an indeterminate number of possible situations and to encourage both responsibility and the ability of individuals, as professionals, to exercise their judgment. A table on those AAA Principles of Professional Responsibility is printed on the inside front cover of this book, spelling out in more detail their key assumptions. In the "Ethical Reasoning" workspaces, you can use that table to guide you through different scenarios and situations to increase your awareness of research ethics.

CRITICAL THINKING • COMMUNICATION

3.2 Ethical Reasoning: Dialing In on "Do No Harm"

The bedrock principle of "do no harm" is common across human-centered fields, including anthropology. But "harm" is a complicated concept, especially for a discipline such as anthropology that recognizes that such a concept can mean different things across cultures. Here the goal is to dial in on some of its subtleties.

Start by reviewing the table on the inside cover.

Define "harm" in your own words:

On the basis of what you know, do you think this definition would apply across cultures? Why or why not?

_____

_____

_____

_____

_____

What kinds of harm do you think fieldwork can produce? (If you don't know, make some educated guesses)

_____

_____

_____

_____

_____

Is there a difference between harm and wrongdoing?

_____

_____

_____

_____

_____

How do you think a can fieldworker can "reduce" harm?

_____

_____

_____

_____

_____

Is there a difference between "do no harm" and "do some good"?

_____

_____

_____

_____

_____

Human Subjects Review and You

Fieldworkers employed in higher education and the federal government typically have to get their research plan approved by a committee in their institution, called an institutional review board (IRB), before they can begin work. Set up in the wake of revelations of clinical and biomedical research abuses such as those mentioned above, the IRB's job is to ensure that federal laws, institutional rules, and ethical guidelines set up to protect the rights and welfare of "human subjects" (participants in a study) are being followed. The fieldworker has to show that a plan (also known as a "protocol") is in place to protect study participants from harm; to ensure that participants know the purpose of the study, their rights if they think they are being harmed, and any risks or benefits they might incur; and to give their **informed consent**, or voluntary and uncoerced permission, to participate in the study. IRB rules apply to research whose goal is to produce generalizable knowledge. Oral histories as well as materials gathered for journalistic purposes (such as unstructured interviews or anecdotes) are not "human-subjects research" according to IRB rules and thus are not subject to review.

If you are taking a class and using this book in it—especially an introductory-level course in cultural anthropology—the likelihood that you will have to go through an institutional review to conduct the activities in it is very slim, since undergraduate coursework is "exempt" from IRB oversight if it is for conventional educational purposes, if it will not be published, if it does not permit participants to be identified, and if it does not involve any "vulnerable" populations (people under 18 years old, prisoners, and various other categories). However, your professor may need to receive blanket permission from the IRB for your course to do some of these exercises. For upper-level courses the same usually applies, but for independent studies and senior theses where there is more-extensive fieldwork being conducted, a student typically will have to undergo an IRB approval process. The best way to familiarize yourself with the rules at your institution is to look at them directly.

3.3   Meeting Your Institution's IRB—A Basic Worksheet

COMMUNICATION

Find your institution's human-subjects research or IRB website and look through it. Find answers to the following and write them here:

What are the types of research projects it reviews?

_____

_____

_____

What guidance does it provide to students doing research for class projects? Summarize the key points here.

_____

_____

_____

What is a "protocol"?

_____

_____

_____

What training and forms are required to submit a "protocol"?

_____

_____

_____

What are the differences among "exempt," "expedited," and "full" review?

_____

_____

_____

Space for Extra Notes

Space for Extra Notes

PART II

DOING FIELDWORK

At some point while doing fieldwork, every anthropologist realizes he or she has been *told* one thing, only to have the same people *do* something different. True, it could be that those people are untrustworthy, or that they are saying what they think the fieldworker wants to hear. But it's usually the case that these different responses were triggered by different situations or contexts. People are not robots, programmed to react inflexibly to the world around them. Moreover, what might seem initially paradoxical can reveal itself, with time and effort on the part of the fieldworker, to be an expression of a subtle cultural logic, social pattern, or set of motives playing out in a particular context.

This kind of situation points to one reason that fieldwork methods are not limited to one set of techniques or data sources such as surveys or interviews. Even while those techniques can produce useful data, in isolation they miss crucial contextual details about people's actions and meanings that a complementary technique such as observation or experiential participation might better pick up. Different methodological techniques reveal different things, and the research techniques a fieldworker uses shape what he or she experiences and knows. Also, data created using one method can shed light on data created using another. Learning how to produce a trustworthy account of the cultural lives of others involves knowing the appropriate conditions under which one technique might generate useful data, checking the reliability of those data against data created using other techniques, and then identifying patterns that emerge out of the diverse types of data that have been created. All these things are rooted in building unique, trusting relationships with people participating in the research. The goal of this section is to give you a practical introduction to the range of techniques on which fieldworkers draw to do these things.

CHAPTER FOUR

TAKING NOTES

In answer to the question "What do anthropologists do?," the influential anthropologist Clifford Geertz (Geertz 1973) responded, "They write." Perhaps to the beginner this is an odd way to characterize a discipline in which the experience-rich activity of fieldwork plays a central role. But thinking about *what* and *how* to write about those rich experiences, and then actually doing it, are critical elements of the fieldwork process. Fieldwork is, in significant respects, *participating in order to write* (Emerson et al. 2011).

By recording what we observe, hear, and experience, anthropologists create most of the texts we will later work with in order to write up our research. To an important extent, taking notes is a practical matter of getting down on paper various details of social interaction and snippets of conversation so we don't forget them. Field notes are thus a means to an end, an essential ingredient in jogging and correcting our memories when analyzing and writing about the details of people's lives after fieldwork is concluded. Because they are proxies for memory, fieldworkers spend a lot of time working on their field notes, often tearing themselves away from the flow of social life to do it. Taking good notes requires a lot of discipline and time. But it is not always clear if everything that is recorded will be analytically useful later, so one has to have faith that all that effort is worth it.

But note taking is also not simply a mechanical matter. It is an act of interpretation and sense making by the fieldworker. The quality of a fieldworker's relationships with others will affect what goes into them, as well as how and when he or she writes them (Emerson et al. 2011). Because we cannot record everything we experience and observe, every fieldworker makes decisions about what is significant or insignificant, focusing on certain stories, events, or comments while missing others altogether. The things recorded in field notes are fragments of

KEY RESOURCE. Two key books on note taking include Roger San-jek's *Fieldnotes: The Makings of Anthropology* (Sanjek 1990) and Robert Emerson, Rachel Fretz, and Linda Shaw's *Writing Ethnographic Fieldnotes* (Emerson et al. 2011). The first book is more historical and philosophical essays; the second is a practical guide.

complex social lives, based on fleeting incidents or conversations, yet they constitute the social world we will ultimately share with others (Emerson et al. 2011).

Field notes can be taken contemporaneously (while an event or conversation is happening), although this can make people uncomfortable. Most people will usually get used to note taking (some, such as experts or leaders, might even expect it), but fieldworkers also do a lot of note taking immediately or soon after an incident, when it's less disruptive and easier to concentrate. As an explicit "research" activity, note taking identifies the fieldworker socially in a community as "a researcher," which in certain instances can be strategically useful to play up (such as with authority figures who welcome or even expect others to take notes on what they say and do) and in others to play down (such as when wanting to participate fully in community events or activities, when note taking can be disruptive).

The audience for notes is typically the fieldworker's "future self," which is to say the self down the road who will be using those notes to craft an ethnographic account (Emerson et al. 2011). As a result, most fieldworkers think of their notes as personal documents, writing them without aiming to achieve the rhetorical elegance, consistency, and sharpness they will strive for in more-formal writings. Different fieldworkers write notes differently, and there is a lot of room for personal style in note taking (figure 4.1).

And yet, experienced fieldworkers also know that some notes are better than others. Principles of good note taking include (adapted and modified from Emerson et al. 1995: 32–33):

- **Jot down some background.** Write some of the key components of the scene, such as date, time of day, setting, who is there, and any other features that might stand out.
- **Show, don't tell.** Be concrete, closely describing what people are doing, and using actual words and phrases people use. Describe instead of summarize.
- **Avoid generalizing.** Avoid impressionistic words ("incredible," "vague," etc.) and opinions ("bad," "horrible," "strange," etc.), both of which allow you to make generalizations, which you shouldn't be doing at this stage.
- **Avoid projecting internal states and emotions.** You don't know how someone feels inside, or a person's motives. For example, what you

might interpret as someone's anger, frustration, or feelings of insecurity may actually be something else. It's better to write down *how* and potentially *why* such emotions might be expressed.

- **Jot down any sensory details and intuitions you might have.** Recognizing that a key goal of field notes is to jog and correct our memories later, little details of the scene—sights, smells, sounds, your emotional reactions, and so on—could help you remember details, and your intuitions could point to important issues for further research.
- **Keep a running list of questions.** You should jot down questions that come to mind, to inquire into later or as a follow-up question if you are conducting an interview. Many fieldworkers will mark off an area

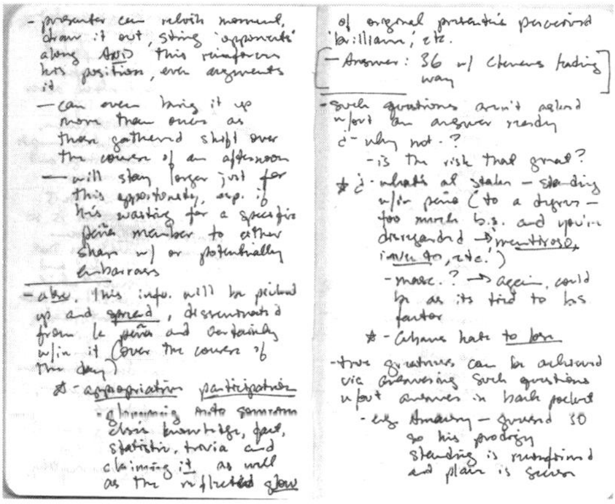

(a)

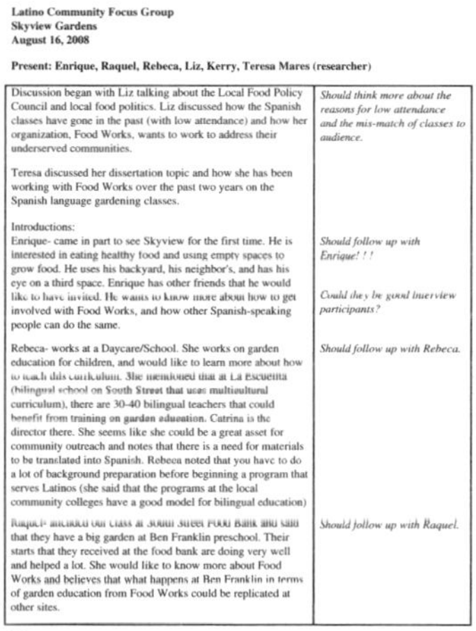

Latino Community Focus Group
Skyview Gardens
August 16, 2008

Present: Enrique, Raquel, Rebeca, Liz, Kerry, Teresa Mares (researcher)

Discussion began with Liz talking about the Local Food Policy Council and local food politics. Liz discussed how the Spanish classes have gone in the past (with low attendance) and how her organization, Food Works, wants to work to address their underserved communities. Teresa discussed her dissertation topic and how she has been working with Food Works over the past two years on the Spanish language gardening classes.	*Should think more about the reasons for low attendance and the mis-match of classes to audience.*
Introductions: Enrique- came in part to see Skyview for the first time. He is interested in eating healthy food and using empty spaces to grow food. He uses his backyard, his neighbor's, and has his eye on a third space. Enrique has other friends that he would like to have invited. He wants to know more about how to get involved with Food Works, and how other Spanish-speaking people can do the same.	*Should follow up with Enrique! ! !* *Could they be good interview participants?*
Rebeca- works at a Daycare/School. She works on garden education for children, and would like to learn more about how to teach this curriculum. She mentioned that at La Escuelita (bilingual school on South Street that uses multicultural curriculum), there are 30-40 bilingual teachers that could benefit from training on garden education. Catrina is the director there. She seems like she could be a great asset for community outreach and notes that there is a need for materials to be translated into Spanish. Rebeca noted that you have to do a lot of background preparation before beginning a program that serves Latinos (she said that the programs at the local community colleges have a good model for bilingual education)	*Should follow up with Rebeca.*
Raquel- attended our class at South Street Food Bank and said that they have a big garden at Ben Franklin preschool. Their starts that they received at the food bank are doing very well and helped a lot. She would like to know more about Food Works and believes that what happens at Ben Franklin in terms of garden education from Food Works could be replicated at other sites.	*Should follow up with Raquel.*

(b)

FIGURE 4.1 Two Fieldworkers, Two Different Note-Taking Styles. The two anthropologists whose notes appear here mix note taking on action and talking with sense-making reflections, question posing, and notes to themselves.

(a) *Fieldworker*: Ben Eastman (PhD, University of Chicago).
What: Two face-to-face pages in a 3.5 × 5.5-inch black Moleskine notebook.
Note-taking strategy: In this excerpt from his fieldwork on the relationship between baseball and the state in post-socialist Cuba, Eastman recorded raw notes on a conversation and then (halfway through the page on the left) pulls back, shifting toward analytical reflections. On the right-hand page, he poses several questions for further reflection and investigation.

(b) *Fieldworker*: Teresa Mares (PhD, University of Washington).
What: 8.5 × 11-inch page, typewritten using laptop.
Note-taking strategy: In this excerpt from her fieldwork on foodways of Latino migrants in Seattle, Mares produced these typed notes based on jot notes and head notes taken during the meeting she records here. Note that Mares uses a standard template that divides the page vertically, with questions and notes to herself separated from notes about things directly observed or heard.

FIELDWORK TIP

A Future Self? The "future self" might be several weeks or months off, such as when you sit down to write an end-of-semester project. For professional anthropologists, that self might be *several years* off in the future. An experienced fieldworker knows that the notes need to have a lot of concrete detail and background since many details will be forgotten by then.

in the margins of the paper where these questions go so they are separate from the field notes, such as one of the field note examples in figure 4.1.

Keep these points in mind as you undertake all the exercises in this chapter, which are designed to introduce you to the basics. But good note taking requires a lot of practice! So as you work through exercises in later chapters, come back to this list to evaluate how well you are following these principles.

4.1   Notes on Action

ACCURACY AND ATTENTION TO DETAIL

Ask a friend if you can take notes for seven to ten minutes on him or her performing an everyday activity, such as washing dishes, fixing a bike, cooking a meal, looking for a book in the library, or other possibilities. Think of yourself as a fly on the wall for this exercise, and jot down notes here on what you observe while it is happening, following the principles above. Don't worry about getting down what the person might be saying, just focus on describing movements, actions, and effects.

_____

_____

_____

_____

_____

_____

_____

_____

_____

_____

Developing a note-taking style that works best for you involves balancing the principles listed above with your own intentional approach. That approach develops by tweaking how you might already structure notes (such as how you take lecture notes in class), growing your descriptive vocabulary, refining a personal shorthand of symbols and abbreviations, and—quite simply—learning by doing.

Because a fieldwork project can create a lot of notes, it is also important to have a system for organizing field notes. It is critical to date or time-stamp notes, and it is helpful to have a short description at the top of what is in the notes. Some fieldworkers annotate their notes more fully after they are finished writing them, adding questions, comments, and any preliminary analytic thinking. Notes can be organized by day or by theme or in physical or electronic folders on a laptop, but the overarching goal is logical organization for easy retrieval.

"Head Notes": Remembering, Elaborating, and Filling In from Memory

It is likely that in the previous exercise you couldn't get down exactly what happened, and in fact even good notes don't capture everything that transpired exactly as it did. At the same time, there are always comments, postures, interactions, and subtle incidents we saw or heard but didn't write down. These memories are called **head notes**, and they can occur to us hours, maybe even days, later, and it's important to get them down too (Ottenberg 1990). The more the fieldworker knows about a research setting, the greater the quantity of head notes. Remembering, elaborating, and filling in head note details after the fact adds useful layers of detail to field notes.

Many fieldworkers record their head notes in the margins of their raw jottings, or more likely when they convert their raw jottings into a longer-hand treatment. The idea is to "return to the scene" and type up or rewrite the raw notes, adding details that weren't in them, elaborating on what was observed or heard, and expanding the description with any relevant background, explanations, qualifications, and so on (figure 4.2). When fieldworkers are working so hard on their field notes, it is often because they are converting those raw jottings to fuller notes.

Notes on Spoken and Nonverbal Communication

Since a major goal of fieldwork is to try to understand what people think in their own terms and the meanings they give to things, fieldworkers also take

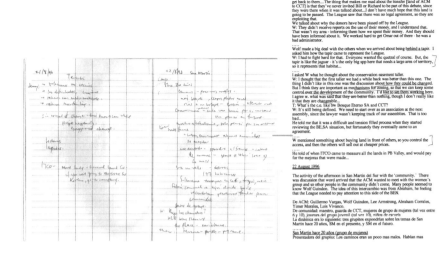

FIGURE 4.2 Field Notes, from "Raw" to "Cooked." Many fieldworkers convert raw notes taken in notebooks to more-detailed, or "cooked," typewritten notes. This example, from my field notes created while researching environmentalism in rural Costa Rica, were initially taken using shorthand in a 5x7-inch all-weather scientific field notebook (*left*). Within 24 hours they were rewritten and expanded on using a laptop (*right*). Some of these interviews were conducted in English and others were in Spanish, and I recorded them in their original language.

FIELDWORK TIP

Adding Head Notes. Up to a day after you've completed any individual exercise in this chapter, go back to it and add any head notes. Use a different-color pen or have some notation that indicates it's a head note. Make those notes wherever there is space—in the margins or edges of the paper—but be sure to make arrows to where in the flow of events your head note refers to.

notes on conversations and spoken interactions. The goal of taking notes on talking is to write down as much of the actual phrasing and words as possible and *not to summarize what people say*, because it imposes too much of our own language and interpretation. It is also important to clearly differentiate between speakers when multiple people are talking, and fieldworkers develop notations so that later they know who said what. In this exercise, you will try taking notes on a conversation between two people.

4.2 Notes on Talking

For this exercise you will need two people who are willing to let you sit in on a five- to seven-minute conversation about anything while you take notes. You should preferably not work with close friends, but distant relations or strangers. Another option is to do this exercise using a video recording of a movie or television talk show with two people having a conversation for at least five minutes. An excellent resource is a movie titled *The Trip* (Winterbottom 2010), which involves extended scenes of conversation between friends (if not accessible through your library, it is available to stream through Netflix). If you use a video, do not stop it to write down what you miss; if working with people, don't ask them to repeat what they said. The goal here is to get down what you can about what the individuals are saying, using any shorthand, symbols, and abbreviations that make sense to you. It's recommended that you also have a shorthand way of alternating between speakers, such as using their initials when they begin speaking so you later know who said what.

When taking notes on a conversation or other spoken discourse, it is also important to take notes on interactional details, such as body language, facial expressions, use of physical space, and physical responses. Nonverbal communication can often reveal subtleties of attitude and relationship that are not reflected in spoken words. Most experienced fieldworkers would integrate these details into a transcript of a spoken dialogue, but the goal of the next exercise is to focus just on nonverbal communication to help you get accustomed to its subtleties.

4.3 Notes on Nonverbal Communication

If you used a video such as *The Trip*, turn off the sound of the segment you took notes on and record body language, expression, how individuals use personal space, etc., paying especially close attention to changes in these conditions. After you are done, see if you can line up the nonverbal details with the transcript in 4.2. If you worked with actual people, it might not be possible to do this exercise; instead, simply observe a natural conversation between people and jot down just the nonverbal aspects of their communication.

ACCURACY AND ATTENTION TO DETAIL

_____

_____

_____

_____

_____

_____

_____

_____

_____

_____

_____

_____

_____

_____

_____

_____

_____

_____

_____

_____

_____

_____

_____

_____

4.4   Reflections on Note Taking

Go back and examine the contents of your notes in exercises 4.1, 4.2, and 4.3. Think about the process of taking those notes. Which one felt easiest to take notes on, and which was more difficult? Is there anything you would do differently the next time you take notes?

_____

_____

_____

_____

_____

_____

_____

_____

_____

_____

_____

_____

_____

_____

_____

_____

_____

_____

_____

_____

_____

_____

_____

_____

Other Kinds of Notes

A growing body of field notes is often characterized by disconnected events, conversations, observations, and other fragments of data. Although in the early stages of research it may feel that the notes are all over the place, reflecting "an attempt to vacuum up everything possible" (Agar 1996: 154), as the project advances and becomes more focused the notes should become more specific (see chapter 12). Further, adding more-extended field note entries can create greater coherence. As described in Emerson et al. 2011, these extended entries can include:

- **Sketches**: Description of a scene, setting, individual, or incident with vivid details. Intentionally impressionistic. A written form of "still life" with no chronology or plot.

- **Episodes**: Extended recounting of a string of actions, interactions, or incidents. Chronology is important. If detailed enough, it might reveal certain patterns or raise certain questions for further research.

- **Field note tales**: A more elaborate narrative that combines sketches and episodes, but not necessarily polished. Typically story driven.

In addition, fieldworkers don't just write their own documents, they collect them too. These include published or unpublished reports, internal organizational documents, newspaper clippings, and other formal and informal writings written by others related to the research. As a fieldworker works through those documents to understand what's in them and begins to analyze them, it is normal to jot down notes about them as well.

NEGOTIATION • COMMUNICATION

4.5 Ethical Reasoning: Protecting Your Notes

Review the "protect and preserve your records" principle in the table on the inside cover. What are some reasons you might want to ensure the security and confidentiality of raw data?

How do you think you could ensure these things?

What is the point of preserving field notes beyond their usefulness for a particular project?

Under what conditions might it be acceptable for someone besides yourself to gain access to your field notes?

_____

_____

_____

_____

FIELDWORK TIP

Practical Strategies for Ethical Note Taking.

- Remove identifying information about people you are observing or interviewing.
- Use pseudonyms for individuals instead of actual names.
- Try not to include details about individuals that could allow them to be identified if somebody sees your notes.
- Keep your notes in a password-protected computer file or locked file cabinet.

Space for Extra Notes

CHAPTER FIVE

OBSERVING

As individuals, many anthropologists think of themselves as "people watchers." We are curious about what people around us are doing, keeping an eye on the routines of others while going through our daily lives, and at other times content to pull back altogether and watch from the sidelines. This bearing of alertness and curiosity about others is a critical aspect of doing fieldwork. But moving from people watching as a casual orientation to observation as a prolonged and systematic research strategy requires intentionality and critical understanding about different observational strategies.

Observing naturally occurring situations, interactions, and everyday activities is one of qualitative fieldwork's most important techniques. But there is no single approach to doing it. Observational strategies exist along a continuum between direct observation, or a fly-on-the-wall perspective that avoids or limits interacting with others, to immersive participation in a social activity or community. Between these poles exist improvisational and contextually sensitive approaches of participant-observation that combine various modes of watching and doing. In a long-term project a fieldworker might use all these strategies, employing a specific approach for a particular situation.

	CHARACTERISTICS AND USES	COMPLICATIONS AND LIMITATIONS
Direct observation Fly-on-the-wall	Good for recording close detail and data on behavior. Focuses on outward behaviors, often expressed in public. Can be structured to focus on a very specific issue.	Can make people uncomfortable because it can seem like eavesdropping. No necessary connection between observer and observed. Emphasizes researcher as stranger. Limited insights into cultural meanings.
Observation-participation Participation-observation	Improvisational strategies of observing and participating, emphasizing one mode over another or trying to strike a balance between them. Can create useful firsthand experience and embodied knowledge about a process or event, especially those visible only to cultural insiders. Can create (but also relies on) rapport and interactivity with study participants. Unstructured and responsive to flow of events.	Observational data are result of individual experience so can be difficult to generalize. Can be difficult to maintain professional distance.
Participation	Full immersion in community, living and participating as any "native" does. Good for developing experiential insights, feelings, and intuitions about another way of life.	Certain professional concerns—such as note taking or maintaining some personal distance—downplayed. Raises important ethical questions because the researcher does not necessarily disclose, or participants in the project forget, that "research" is taking place.

When making observations, fieldworkers usually begin by casting their nets broadly, recording a range of details about the scene and fragments of talk or action. This provides some orientation to what's going on and can help identify any elements that stand out. Later, more attention can be given to a specific issue or concern, as you'll see in this direct-observation exercise.

5.1 Direct Observation in a Public Space

FIELDWORK TIP

A Team Approach. If you have the opportunity, doing a direct observation such as this as a team activity with three or four others is an excellent opportunity to expand your sense of what is happening, as well as to discuss the particularities of experience and perspective that each individual brings to the table. Compare your notes when you are finished.

Identify a public space—if you are on campus, you could go to a dining hall, the library, a student lounge, or a sports event. Off-campus options might be a restaurant, a shopping mall, or a park. Conduct your observation during a time when there is activity taking place so you have enough to observe. If anybody asks what you're doing, tell them, but otherwise don't interact, just observe. Decide on a position from which to observe the space—think about what it will help you see (and not see). Take notes on your observations here. You should do the following:

- Begin by jotting down some details about the physical setting, what people are doing here, and where you are situated.

- Describe in detail the activity you are observing—remember the principles of good note taking (concreteness, describing not summarizing, etc.). Focus on action, interaction, movement, and effect. Pay attention to sounds and smells. You can also include snippets of overheard conversation.

- As you observe, begin to focus on something that interests you, such as a pattern that emerges or a peculiar activity that captures your attention.

After 30 minutes of observation and note taking here, stop. Don't forget to add any marginal headnotes, questions that emerged for you, intuitions, and so on.

DIRECTED LEARNING • CURIOSITY • ATTENTION TO DETAIL AND ACCURACY

_____

_____

_____

_____

_____

One of the primary challenges of observing is knowing where to focus attention, which can be difficult even when there is not a lot going on. Having a goal for your observations helps greatly. You should always be open to what the scene unfolding before you presents—unexpected conflicts, compelling interactions or individuals, and other dynamics. But deciding ahead of time on a focus can make the difference between feeling overwhelmed to the point

FIELDWORK TIP

Shadowing. Another observational approach is to shadow someone over a period of time (with their permission, of course), following them as they navigate their everyday lives and writing notes about their actions, behaviors, and expressions. This approach can be supplemented with other techniques, such as asking questions and mapping.

of paralysis, and feeling that you have effectively recorded important aspects of social life within your visual horizon. Possibilities for narrowing observations depend on your research questions, but could include the following:

- **A process, transaction, or activity** (e.g., ordering and paying for a sandwich in a dining hall or a meal in a restaurant)
- **A particular place or space** (e.g., the social activity within a room in the library)
- **A particular group of people** (e.g., the home team during its warm-up exercises)
- **A phenomenon** (e.g., how people use space to communicate nonverbally)
- **Particular kinds of social interactions** (e.g., interactions between authority figures and subordinates)
- **Testing a theory** (e.g., "women use public space differently than men")

When there are a lot of people doing things in the space you are observing, general words such as "people," "person," and "student" in your notes are vague and unhelpful. You should always specify details about the "people" you are seeing. Males? Females? With shaved heads? Wearing green winter jackets with vertical yellow stripes? Approximate age? Outward demeanor (tranquil, agitated, etc.)? In other words, you need to add enough distinguishing details so that later, when looking at your notes, you can tell individuals apart and can begin to identify any particular social relationships or patterns between them.

Combining Observation and Participation

Integrating a more participatory approach adds new complications to observing, not least of which is now keeping track of not just what others are up to but also what you are doing, experiencing, sensing, and intuiting. It can also disrupt note taking since you yourself may not want to interrupt what's going on to take notes, and others might find it disruptive if you keep stopping what you are doing to jot things down. If everybody sees you as "a researcher" it might actually be expected for you to take notes, but sometimes the easiest way to manage this dilemma is by taking periodic breaks and stepping out— to "use the bathroom," for example, where you feverishly jot down key ideas, incidents, and sensations that later you will fill in and elaborate on with more detail, supported by your head notes. The next exercise gives you your first opportunity to try participant observation.

5.2   Participating to Observe / Observing to Participate

Identify an activity or setting on campus or in your community in which you can participate, experience, or contribute in some way. This could be attending a public meeting (of a student club, for example), a cafeteria where you order food, or a festival, game, workday, parade, election, or other community event. Do this exercise in a space or with a group you are (more or less) unfamiliar with, since it will help you notice things you might not otherwise notice. Give some thought ahead of time about your orientation: Do you want to participate to observe, or observe to participate (i.e., giving relative weight to one over the other)? What you decide might shape your relative posture and any decisions you make about how to interact with others. If the activity or group is small or private, you should ask any leaders or members if it's okay for you to do this exercise; if it's a big, anonymous public event or space, your work is less likely to disrupt others and it might be more difficult or impractical to get everybody's consent. But again, if anybody asks you what you are doing, be open and honest. Do this activity for 30–45 minutes and jot down notes on it here, and remember your good note-taking strategies.

DIRECTED LEARNING • CURIOSITY • ACCURACY AND ATTENTION TO DETAILS, ADAPTABILITY

_____

_____

_____

_____

_____

_____

_____

_____

_____

_____

5.3   Participant Observation Reflection

Did you "participate to observe" or "observe to participate"? How do you think your relative emphasis of one orientation over the other affected what you saw, learned, or experienced?

_____

_____

_____

_____

_____

_____

Describe how you actually "participated" (e.g., your firsthand experience, involvement, interaction with others, etc.).

_____

_____

_____

_____

_____

_____

Describe how and when you took notes.

_____

_____

_____

_____

_____

What was difficult about this exercise?

_____

_____

_____

_____

_____

_____

Briefly, what new insights did you develop about the community
or activity you were involved in?

_____

_____

_____

_____

_____

The lines between participant observation and full-on participation can
get murky, especially the longer and more deeply involved the fieldworker is in
a community. Head notes become even more critical because as one shifts
toward fuller participation, note taking does not take place during events or
conversations or in the flow of everyday life, but separate from others in the
fieldworker's private space. These notes almost always have to be recon-
structed after the fact, entirely from memory.

FIELDWORK TIP

The Plasticity of Memory. Short-term memory is not a fixed capacity. We
can expand our memories by training our brains how to remember things
using common memorization techniques, such as creating mind maps, as-
sociating what people say or do with familiar locations or concepts, and
learning how to recognize and use synesthetic memories.

5.4   Participating and Taking Notes "After the Fact"

For this exercise, choose a group or setting that *you are already involved in or a member of* on campus or in your community. While attending one of its events or activities, such as a meeting or workday, participate as you normally would. Choose a 20-minute segment in the activity to register "head notes," but don't bring out your notebook. After the event is finished, write detailed notes here about what happened and what was said during that 20-minute segment.

_____

_____

_____

_____

_____

_____

_____

_____

_____

_____

_____

_____

_____

_____

_____

_____

_____

_____

_____

_____

_____

_____

_____

_____

_____

_____

_____

_____

_____

_____

_____

_____

_____

_____

5.5   Ethical Reasoning: Informed Consent . . . and Its Limits

Review the "Obtain informed consent" principle in the table at the front of this book. Typically, informed consent involves describing the purpose of the research, explaining why you have chosen an individual to observe or interview, explaining what that person will experience, stating any potential risks or discomforts, notifying participants they can withdraw from the study at any time, and then securing their consent, either orally or as a signature (your IRB will often dictate which one). But is it always possible to get full consent of everybody in a community? Consider and respond to this scenario: you are invited to observe an intimate ritual involving a dozen or so people and are told by the person conducting it that you should arrive just as it is beginning. It does not give you time to seek informed consent of all the participants. What can you do?

NEGOTIATION • CRITICAL THINKING

_____

_____

_____

_____

Space for Extra Notes

CHAPTER SIX

LISTENING

Living in an era of texting and social media, it seems that many of us don't take much time to listen—*really* listen—to others. Sure, we *hear* others, but listening is not just being on the receiving end of sound. Listening requires another level of focus that involves not just paying attention to what is said but also how it is said. It is an active process of making meaning, assessing what is heard, and responding to others in appropriate ways. Listening well is an essential skill for fieldwork because it aids accurate learning about other people's lives, and, equally important, is a means of creating and maintaining respectful and trusting social relationships.

It goes without saying that when you're listening you're not talking. Nonetheless, *listening well is an active process* that involves these components:

- **Concentration.** Focus on what the other person is saying. Avoid distractions and control those feelings of boredom, hunger, or discomfort you might experience. Resist the urge to doodle.

- **Empathy.** Suspend your preconceived ideas and biases about the person and what she is saying. Try to see things from her point of view.

- **Patience.** Let the individual say things in his way, on his timeline. Avoid the impulse to fill in long pauses or finish sentences—this can stress people out, and you should strive to put them at ease.

- **Focusing on voice and tone.** People use voice pitch, tone, and volume to communicate subtleties or give emphasis. Take note of these variations.

- **Attentiveness to nonverbal communication—yours and theirs.** Pay close attention to the other person's gestures, eye contact, and other physical movements. Use your own body language (nodding your head, using facial expressions, etc.) to express your interest and give feedback to show you are listening.

- **Focusing on ideas, not just words.** While processing all those other things, a good listener is linking bits of information to help identify underlying ideas and patterns of thought.

The exercises that follow will aid you in refining the different skills involved in good listening.

6.1   Listening . . . for What?

List 10 situations that require listening. Examples: getting directions, learning about someone you just met, consoling a friend in distress, listening to music. Next to each, list the requirements of good listening for that situation.

1. _____

2. _____

3. _____

4. _____

5. _____

6. _____

7. _____

8. _____

9. _____

10. _____

COMMUNICATION • ACCURACY AND ATTENTION TO DETAIL • CRITICAL THINKING

Reflection: How and why do those listening requirements differ depending on the situation?

_____

_____

_____

6.2 Concentrate!

Listen to a speech, watch a film clip of a conversation, or have a friend read a short story out loud. Aim for it to last 10–15 minutes. Break it up by stopping a few times and writing a question or two here about what you just heard. If you're concentrating, confusions or wonderings should emerge.

_____

_____

_____

When you are finished listening, consider this and write a few sentences about it: How did variations in voice, tone, or body language of the speaker affect your understanding?

_____

_____

_____

_____

_____

_____

_____

COMMUNICATION • ACCURACY AND ATTENTION TO DETAIL

6.3 Focus, Stop, and Paraphrase

Ask a friend or classmate to tell a five- to seven-minute story about something that happened to him or her. Resist any temptation to respond while the person is talking. When she or he stops talking, paraphrase what your friend just said: "You believe that . . . ," "You aren't sure if . . . ," and so on. Write here about any underlying ideas from the story that came out in this exercise.

_____

_____

_____

COMMUNICATION

Reflection: What challenges did you encounter doing this paraphrasing and how might you overcome those challenges? If you did not find this especially challenging, see if you can explain why. Reconstruct what you actually did while listening (concentration on words, focus on body language, eye contact, etc.). What factors might prevent you from listening like this in other circumstances?

_____

_____

_____

_____

_____

_____

_____

_____

_____

_____

Acoustic Environments

Listening is not just a technique for interacting with others and understanding what they have to say. It is also a means of learning about a place and its social dynamics. Human activities and social patterns contribute to the creation of specific acoustic environments. Some of those sounds may be deliberately produced, while others may be improvised, unintentional, or fortuitous (Samuels et al. 2010). Although most people are not continuously or always consciously aware of their acoustic environments, the patterns of sound in any community reflect particular relationships between sound and place and in turn influence people's experience, perceptions, beliefs, and behaviors about their social environment (Feld 1996). Anthropologists interested in the "sounded" dimensions of a community often use field recording equipment to capture ambient sounds and voices as they occur in social settings. They might then create digital "sound maps" (see chapter 8) to identify the spatial distribution of certain sounds, or to analyze how certain sounds are connected to broader social patterns, political-economic processes, and ideologies.

6.4   Take a Soundscape "Listening Tour"

Identify three distinct spaces on or off campus (possibilities include a library, cafeteria, restaurant, park, or other space). Spend about 10–15 minutes in each space and, while there, listen carefully to the sounds you hear. Write some basic notes here about what you are listening to in each space. If you have access to digital sound-recording equipment, you could also record these for playback and analysis.

_____

_____

_____

Reflection: Compare and contrast the sonic characteristics of these spaces.

_____

_____

_____

_____

_____

_____

_____

_____

_____

_____

_____

_____

_____

_____

_____

_____

_____

ACCURACY AND ATTENTION TO DETAIL • ADAPTABILITY • CRITICAL THINKING

_____

_____

_____

How do you think the sounds you were listening to reflect—and
influence—the social activities or experience an individual might
have in these spaces?

_____

_____

_____

_____

_____

6.5   Ethical Reasoning: The Ethics of Eavesdropping

COMMUNICATION • NEGOTIATION • CRITICAL THINKING

Do you think that listening to others without their knowledge
constitutes ethical fieldwork practice? Why (and under what
conditions) or why not?

_____

_____

_____

_____

_____

_____

_____

_____

_____

_____

_____

CHAPTER SEVEN

ASKING QUESTIONS

In addition to observing and listening, asking questions is the lifeblood of ethnographic field methods. As a strategy of directed learning, it is critical for eliciting information, explanations, oral histories, and other spoken data—although, realistically speaking, it is impossible to record *everything exactly* that is said or done while interviewing somebody. As is the case for listening, it is also a means of creating and maintaining social relationships, because most people respond favorably to respectful inquiries and curiosity about their lives.

When asking questions, you should always be sensitive to context, knowing *what* to ask *when*. Your relationship with the respondent, the presence of other people, what the respondent is doing at the time, what you want to know about, the formality or informality of the interaction, and so on—all these factors will shape how you ask questions and the kind of answers you get. The more you know a community and its norms—not to mention the individuals you are interviewing—the easier it can be to know what to ask when, though oftentimes you just won't know these things until you begin asking questions. Moreover, there are different approaches to asking questions, including the following:

- **Surveys.** The researcher creates the questions and gives fixed responses from which respondents choose. The researcher or respondent fills in a form, which typically is used to create quantitative data and support the use of statistical methods to identify generalizable patterns. Survey data are "thin" and unidimensional, and if such data play a role in ethnographic research at all, it is usually to produce baseline data (e.g., income distribution, residency patterns) that is often followed up with qualitative methods.

- **Structured or formal interview.** The researcher works from a list of previously prepared questions, assuming he or she knows the important questions to ask. To ensure consistency across interviews, the researcher goes over the exact questions and sequence of questioning for each interview but does not assume that he or she knows the possible responses. Notes are taken, an audio recording is made, or both, to later transcribe into an interview script.

- **Open-ended interview.** The researcher wants to cover certain general topics and issues, loosely guiding the interview. There is no particular order or manner in which questions are asked, and new questions emerge during the interview. Notes, head notes, or an audio recording are taken. Oral histories, which are interviews focused on an individual's personal experience of a historical process or situation, typically follow an open-ended style of questioning.

- **Informal conversation and hanging out.** Informal conversational exchange or hanging out, in which questions emerge from immediate interactions and context. It rarely feels like a "research event" or even an interview, and note taking is often deemphasized in favor of head notes.

- **Group interviews.** During fieldwork, many interviews are conducted one on one because the individual has particular knowledge or perspective that the fieldworker wants to learn about. But sometimes fieldworkers conduct group interviews of three, four, or more people because there is a spontaneous gathering or a deliberate invitation, such as to a **focus group**. Although they aren't as "natural" as informal interviewing and hanging out, one benefit of a group interview is that participants can respond to each other and generate interactive conversation.

Beginning fieldworkers often assume they should integrate a survey into their research, if for no other reason than it feels like "objective research." But from the vantage point of ethnographic fieldwork, one of the limitations of surveys (which applies to structured interviews as well) is the assumption that the researcher knows what questions to ask and the order in which to ask them. This assumption can get in the way of comprehending tacit native categories, assumptions, and meanings. One of the goals of asking questions in ethnographic fieldwork is to get people talking and telling stories, letting them shape or coshape the conversation to allow for their assumptions to come through. As a result, ethnographic fieldworkers tend to rely heavily on open-ended interviews and informal conversations.

FIELDWORK TIP

To Record or Not to Record . . . That Is the Question. Many fieldworkers selectively audio-record important interviews with a digital or tape recorder. But there are pros and cons of using an audio recorder, and when they use one, experienced fieldworkers do not rely on it alone, often taking notes alongside the recording.

PROS	CONS
Can accurately record talking.	Misses contextual details, nonverbal communication.
Once the interview is transcribed, it can be shared with respondents as a gift for their collaboration, or to generate further opportunities for questions.	Audio recorders fail, batteries die, microphones get clogged with moisture or dust, or sound is garbled because of background noise or poor recorder placement.
Formally marks it as a research event, which can support the fieldworker's identity as a researcher, and the respondent's role in the research project.	It might be socially inappropriate or risky for respondents to have their voices captured on a recording.
	A recorder can be disruptive or distracting both for the fieldworker and interviewee.
	Transcription is labor intensive. Fully transcribing a long interview usually takes longer than the interview itself, since good transcriptions also require extra notes about nonverbal communication.

Asking Questions to Get People Talking

So how does a fieldworker actually ask questions to get people talking? There are a number of considerations:

- **Establish comfort and be clear about your intentions.** Explain why you requested the interview (which you probably already did when you asked for it in the first place, but you can elaborate now) and what you plan to do with the material it generates, and let the respondent know how long it should take. Receive informed consent.

- **Be prepared.** If someone is generous enough to sit down for a formal interview, don't waste his or her time—make sure you are prepared

FIELDWORK TIP

Solicited vs. Unsolicited Accounts. On occasions, fieldworkers realize that soliciting an account by asking questions can be disruptive, threatening, or inappropriate. Here a fieldworker benefits by shifting toward a stance of listening. In their everyday lives, people talk to each other about important matters, and a sensitive fieldworker will realize that it is often not even necessary to formally solicit an account through interviewing (Hammersely and Atkinson 1995).

with questions and issues to cover, and strive to keep it focused on the themes of your research.

- **If it's an informal interview, have a mental framework on which to hang your questions.** Sometimes opportunities emerge spontaneously to conduct an informal interview, and other times reading questions from a list during an interview may feel disruptive. Develop a sense what of questions you'd ask ahead of time and the order you would ask them in. For example, in informal interviews I typically have a general sense ahead of time of what I want to know, but I mentally hang the flow of my questions during the actual interview on a loose "past-present-future" framework. Starting with the past, my goal is to ask several questions about each period, ensuring that before I move on to the next one I've satisfied my curiosity or exhausted my questions. Although nobody can tell the future, I still ask about it because it reflects hopes, values, and intentional plans.

- **Recognize that good questions come in different flavors.** There are different categories of questions that can elicit useful data. These include the following (adapted from Spradley 1979):
  - > **Questions that ask for generalities.** Asking about what's "typical," such as "Tell me about a typical day in your life," or "What kinds of tasks do you generally perform in your job?"
  - > **Questions about experience.** Asking about specific personal experiences, such as "Could you tell me about how you felt when . . . ?" or "What was it like to live through . . . (event, situation, etc.)?"
  - > **Detail-oriented questions.** Often posed as follow-up questions, such as "Could you explain what was happening in your life when . . . ?" or "Can you give an example of . . . ?"

> 👍 **KEY RESOURCE.** James Spradley's *The Ethnographic Interview* (Spradley 1979) is a classic resource on ethnographic interviewing techniques.

> > **Questions that elicit native categories.** Asking questions about how an individual refers to or conceptualizes something, such as "How do you refer to . . . ?" or "What is the difference between a . . . and a . . . ?"

> > **Questions that ask for stories.** Asking individuals to tell you stories about what you're interested in learning, such as "Can you tell me a story about . . . ?" Even people who aren't great storytellers often like to tell stories, and letting them decide what stories they'd like to tell reveals their assumptions about what might be important, poignant, funny, insightful, and so on.

- **Know how to actually frame a good question.** There is no magical recipe to constructing good questions, but avoid questions that elicit a "yes" or "no" answer, which don't lead a respondent to elaborate. Questions starting with "why" should be used with caution, especially if they lead respondents to speculate about something they don't know about. Instead, construct questions around concrete and specific issues respondents are likely to know about and elaborate on, using constructions such as "What do you think about . . . ?," "How do you . . . ?," or "Tell me about . . . ." Be aware of biased language or leading questions and use neutral expressions. For example, asking "Why do you support the death tax?" (code among American political conservatives for estate taxes) is too leading; instead, ask something such as "What do you think about estate taxes?"

- **Use direct questions with caution, and "ask around" the central issues that interest you.** You will always have some specific questions to ask directly, usually to elicit certain information or details. But approaching things directly can unintentionally lead a respondent to provide the kind of answer that reflects what you think and not what he or she means. Or it will give you an unsatisfyingly brief answer, especially if the respondent hasn't given much thought to the issue. So, for example, in my own research on the meanings of environmentalism in Latin America, I have rarely asked people directly, "Why are you an environmentalist?" This assumes that (1) the person thinks of herself that way (she may not), and (2) there is an agreed-upon idea of what "an environmentalist" is. Instead, my questions probe around the topic, such as

"When and why did you get involved in the environmental group?" or "Can you think of a time when you disagreed with something the environmental group did? Can you explain why you disagree?"

- **Ask questions with networking in mind**. An important way to find out who is in a social network is to ask respondents about it. Fieldworkers often ask such things as "Who else was involved?" or "Who else can I talk to to learn more about this?" Sometimes called a "snowball" method of recruiting participants in the research, following up with interview requests to those new individuals expands the fieldworker's social network as well.

- **Know how to keep it going.** Remember to be patient when you are listening, to allow an individual time to compose a response. But when things really slow down, enthusiasm wanes, or a lag appears, you can double back on things said previously and ask follow-up questions ("Can you explain why you reacted that way?" "What happened next?"). Also, pay attention to repeated words—usually they indicate something significant to the individual—and follow up with questions about the issue to which they refer.

- **Know when to stop.** Try to stick to the time frame you indicated at the outset, but also be willing to cut it short—or go longer—in response to enthusiasm, body language, or any other interpersonal or external dynamics. Make sure you give profuse thanks, maybe even a gift—not only is someone being generous in helping you out, but leaving on good terms can help if you want to ask more questions later.

Whom to Interview?

Just as important as knowing how to ask good questions is knowing whom to put them to. Although the selection of interviewees tends to evolve and get more focused over the course of a project, strategic fieldworkers generally look for these types of people:

Gatekeepers	Formal or informal social leaders. In addition to usually knowing a lot about what you're interested in, going through gatekeepers can help identify others to interview and can lend legitimacy to the fieldwork itself. Sometimes it is necessary to go through gatekeepers first; other times it's not entirely clear who the gatekeeper is. Some gatekeepers may try to control and shape the research.
Self-selected individuals	Talkative individuals forward about sharing their concerns and perspectives, or those individuals closely tied to your research topic who demonstrate interest in your project. Be aware that sometimes they are doing it because they have a particular agenda.

Reflective individuals	Observant, thoughtful people who are sometimes at the margins or are outsiders in their own social setting.
Knowledge keepers	Individuals associated with a certain body of knowledge. Interviews of these individuals are often direct and focused, yielding specific details about particular issues or concerns.

Is it important to select interviewees who provide a "representative sample" of the community? In general, it is better to hear from more, not fewer, people, but it also depends on the research questions. For some projects, it can be useful to understand the heterogeneity and range of ideas, experiences, and perspectives within a population. It is also important to "triangulate" what people tell you; that is, to test and verify the details of what you are told with other people. But it's not always clear what the boundaries of the population actually are, and fieldworkers usually just have to do their best to achieve representativeness by comparing who is selected for interviews with what is known about the population more generally (Hammersley and Atkinson 1995).

7.1 Asking Good Questions

This exercise has two parts. In the first, a fieldwork scenario is briefly presented, followed up with some interview questions to model good question asking. In the second part, you will fill in the questions.

Part 1. You are doing fieldwork on concepts and experiences of bodily discipline and suffering among members of your college's cycling team. You have set up an interview with the team captain to learn about the team's training regimen. You might want to ask these sorts of questions:

- Who plans and runs team trainings? What are the goals of a training session?

- What kind of training do team members do outside of team practices?

- Can you describe a typical team training ride?

- During a training ride, how do team members show they're experiencing physical or emotional difficulties, and how do other team members respond? How do you respond?

- Is there a team member who has had an especially trying time with an injury or other problem? Do you think I could talk to him or her?

DIRECTED LEARNING • ASKING GOOD QUESTIONS • NETWORKING

COMMUNICATION • WORKING WITH DIFFERENCE

Part 2. Develop good interview questions for each of these scenarios.

(a) You are doing fieldwork on interactions between student government and university administration to understand campus power relationships. You have set up an interview with a member of the student senate. What five questions would you ask?

_____

_____

_____

(b) You are doing fieldwork in a grocery store in your community to study labor conditions for women workers. You have set up an interview with a middle-aged woman who is a cashier. What five questions would you ask?

_____

_____

_____

(c) Take a semester fieldwork project you are currently planning, or dream one up. Briefly explain your project focus here and one person you plan to interview. What five questions will you ask?

_____

_____

_____

7.2 Guiding an Informal Interview

DIRECTED LEARNING • ASKING GOOD QUESTIONS

As noted above, it can be useful in an informal interview to hang the flow of your questions on a mental framework, guiding the interview through general topics and questions while letting questions also emerge in the moment. The past-present-future structure is one useful way to do it. Come up with three general questions for each period that you could ask in an interview for a project you are working on (or dream up a project that interests you).

Past:

Present:

Future:

Can you think of another mental framework you could hang interview questions on besides the past-present-future structure? Explain its advantages.

• COMMUNICATION • CRITICAL THINKING

_____

_____

_____

_____

_____

_____

_____

7.3   Structured vs. Informal Interviews

Here is your chance to use those interview questions you came up with in 7.2. Find the individual, classmate, or stranger whom you want to pose those questions to and request an interview. Aim for it to take about 20 to 30 minutes. Make sure you start with an explanation of what to expect, and ask for informed consent. (1) Start by doing a structured interview in which you keep this notebook open, follow your questions, and write the notes here. (2) Halfway through, close this book and shift toward an informal approach in which you do not consult the questions directly; let questions emerge as you go, and ask follow-up questions. Don't take notes, but write them here after your interview is over.

DIRECTED LEARNING • ASKING GOOD QUESTIONS • NETWORKING • COMMUNICATION

_____

_____

_____

_____

_____

_____

_____

_____

_____

Part 1: Structured interview (taken contemporaneously).

WORKING WITH DIFFERENCE

Part 2: Informal Interview (written after the fact as head notes).

_____

_____

_____

_____

_____

_____

7.4 Ethical Reasoning: Ethical Interviewing

Generally speaking, ethical interviewing requires the fieldworker to hold the interview in a place agreeable and safe to the interviewee, to provide a guarantee of confidentiality, and to receive permission to audio record, publish results, or both (typically received in the form of informed consent). Aside from these generalities, do you think there are other factors in ethical interviewing? For example, are there certain out-of-bounds questions or things you shouldn't ask? Give examples.

_____

_____

_____

_____

_____

_____

_____

_____

_____

_____

_____

_____

_____

_____

_____

_____

CHAPTER EIGHT

MAPPING

The use of space is an important aspect of culture. In any community, the location of resources, who sits where at important social functions, the relative placement and architecture of buildings and structures, and the places where daily tasks are performed influence and are shaped by the socioeconomic order, everyday social rhythms, and cultural meanings (Kuznar and Werner 2001: 204). In cultural anthropology, creating maps of social spaces has been used mainly as a visual accompaniment to ethnography, but many cultural anthropologists also use mapping as a research tool that can supplement and illuminate field note details (Chapin et al. 2005, Andrews 2012). Not only does mapping alert a fieldworker to subtleties of setting and spatial relationships, it can also refine one's descriptive abilities beyond the realm of textual expression, encouraging the ethnographer to explore and visualize how the built and physical worlds relate to cultural processes.

Cartographers generally emphasize that good maps exhibit these features:

Accuracy	Achieving a completely accurate measurement in a fieldwork setting is rare, if not impossible. So the fieldworker has to decide what degree of accuracy is necessary for the project. Is it inches? Feet? Meters? Miles? It depends on project focus and the scale of the space being mapped—which can range between small, such as an altar or a room, to large, such as a neighborhood, a village, or even a region.
Orientation	Maps should identify the cardinal points, to locate the map in space. Culturally important activities in many societies often correspond to cardinal points.

Scale	Even if it's a line representing what the particular distance in actual space equals on the map, scale is an important map feature.
Datum	A reference point—usually a permanent landscape marker, such as a rock outcrop—that anchors other features on a map.
Legend	If there are any symbols in the map (e.g., rivers, houses), the map should have a labeling system. It could be as simple as a list of graphics in the margins defining what each symbol means.

Thanks to technologies such as handheld GPS (Global Positioning System) units, which can locate coordinates in space, and GIS (Geographic Information Systems), which can create computerized maps with layered details, the possibilities for mapping all kinds of natural and social processes have been expanding. This is not to say that a low-tech approach is necessarily any less promising for a fieldworker. Even informal sketch maps can aid better understanding—and feelings of connection to—a particular space (Andrews 2012) (figure 8.1).

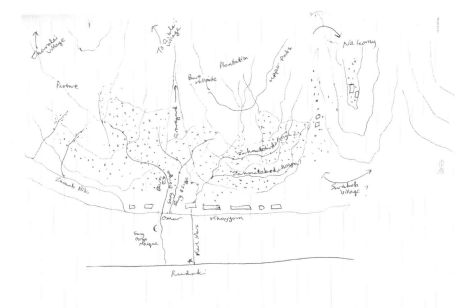

FIGURE 8.1 Mapping for Sense Making.
Fieldworker: Jonah Steinberg (PhD, University of Pennsylvania).
What: 8.5 × 11-inch spiral-bound notebook, hand-drawn map.
Map-making strategy: Steinberg drew this map of the spatial arrangement of migrant households on the mountainous edges of Dushanbe, the capital of Tajikistan. He drew this map partly as a means of not getting lost on returning to conduct interviews, but also as a means to think through a possible article on the development and spatial dynamics of slums in the post-Soviet era.

8.1   Mapping a Space

Choose a city block, campus quad, shopping mall, church/synagogue/ mosque, or similar public or semipublic space. If it is a city block, it can either be a chunk of land bounded on four sides by streets, or the two facing sides of one block of a single street, plus any alleys. If it is a semipublic space, such as a church or mall, make sure you get permission. Sketch a map of the space below using a pencil, and keep in mind the principles above. Try to offer as much detail as possible, but think about why you are choosing certain details over others. At this point, pay more attention to space than activity in it. Describe any traces of human uses of the space (e.g., obvious trash or junk piles, pathways through grass or snow, markings where something is worn by human use). You may want to visit this space at different times of the day or the week, since you may notice different dynamics (light and dark, busy and not busy, etc.).

DIRECTED LEARNING • CURIOSITY • ACCURACY AND ATTENTION TO DETAIL • COMMUNICATION

KEY RESOURCES. This list comes from Kuznar and Werner 2001 and Werner and Kuznar 2001. See also Les Roberts's *Mapping Cultures: Place, Practice, Performance* (Roberts 2012).

Now that you have mapped a space, it is important to think about what a map does and doesn't visualize. With their bird's-eye view, most maps, and probably yours, tend to visualize a space as abstract and static. This is not "wrong," per se, but for the fieldworker researching details of everyday life, it is important to remember that people do not experience, conceptualize, or even visualize any space like a map does. They actively imagine, perform, and dwell in space, and they do it in ways that might be very particular to the place. Moreover, maps do not just "visualize": they can organize space in terms of other sensual frameworks. For example, it is possible to create a map that is based on systematic locating of sounds. A "soundscape map" locates particular meaningful sounds in space, identifying potential locational patterns in sound that might not be immediately apparent to the casual listener.

One of the challenges for ethnographic mapmaking is to introduce social dynamism and cultural meaning into a map. One way to do the former is to add social action and process to the map you created, identifying where certain activities (transactions, interactions, social control, etc.) are taking place. The goal is to look for any patterned relationships between particular physical locations and activities, and to inquire into how and why they are related.

FIELDWORK TIP

Network Mapping. Not all maps are spatial maps. So-called network mapping can visualize relationships between individuals in a social network. Although there are multiple digital tools to create a sophisticated visual model, even a basic social-network sketch can encourage a fieldworker to specify the types of connections between individuals, the distribution of relationships, and group clusters.

8.2 Bringing Your Map to (Social) Life

DIRECTED LEARNING • CURIOSITY • ACCURACY AND ATTENTION TO DETAIL • COMMUNICATION

Photocopy your map above and bring it with you to the space you mapped when you know there will be people and activity there. Observe what people are doing and where they do it. Like any observation exercise, you'll need to focus your observations on something specific. Using colored pencils or some other system that differentiates whom and what you are observing, mark up the map to show patterns of movement or activity. Tape your map here when you are done, and jot down any thoughts you have about what you learned—about the process of bringing social activity into a map, or about the relationship between space and a particular social activity.

Participatory Mapping

Another way to bring dynamism—and more importantly, meaning—into mapping is through a technique called **participatory mapping**, which brings people together to interactively create a visual representation of a space they know well (such as a neighborhood, community, or landscape), by using tools such as paper, pencils, markers, and cameras. While creating a visual representation of the space, members of the group deliberate how best to represent the space and tell personal stories about it, which create opportunities for a fieldworker to listen and take notes on the meanings of the space. Most participatory mapping exercises are deliberately collaborative, can take a while, and are about creating or strengthening group relationships. But not all need to be like this, as you will see in the next exercise.

8.3 An Exercise in Participatory Mapping

DIRECTED LEARNING • CURIOSITY • ACCURACY AND ATTENTION TO DETAIL

On a separate sheet of paper, draw the outlines of your building, campus, town, or physical space in which you are conducting fieldwork, leaving the details blank, and make copies of it. Ask 10 or so individuals who use the space to fill it in with "their" details; that is, the places, activities, routes, and so on that they consider important. Ideally, discuss it with them as they are doing it, pushing them to specify details, and jot down any notes of what they say. Write here about any insights you may have developed about the uses and meanings of space or participatory mapping itself.

_____

_____

_____

_____

_____

_____

_____

_____

_____

_____

_____

_____

_____

_____

_____

_____

_____

_____

_____

_____

_____

_____

_____

_____

_____

_____

_____

_____

_____

_____

_____

• NETWORKING • COMMUNICATION • WORKING WITH DIFFERENCE

8.4 Beyond a "Bird's-Eye View"?

People don't conceive of or interact with the spaces of their daily lives from a bird's-eye view. With a space you know well (such as a dorm room or your bedroom, a campus quad, your car, or a classroom), experiment here with different modes of mapping the space that are not "from above," such as a three-dimensional perspectival map or a panoramic view. What does this visualization help you see that you might not have recognized before?

DIRECTED LEARNING • CURIOSITY

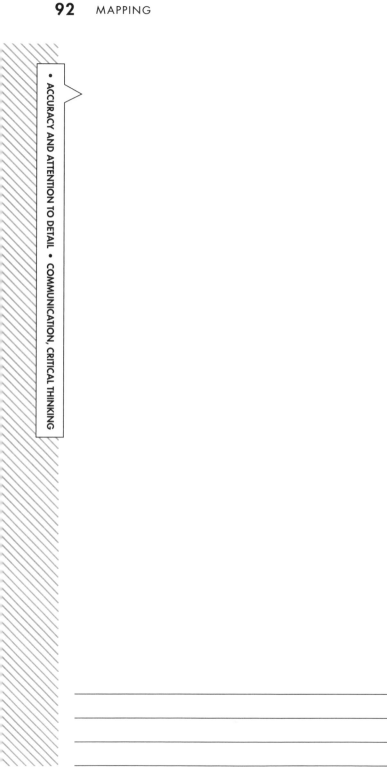

ACCURACY AND ATTENTION TO DETAIL • COMMUNICATION, CRITICAL THINKING

KEY RESOURCES. If you want to see an interesting illustration of a similar process, though its goals are not scholarly ones, see Becky Cooper's book *Mapping Manhattan: A Love (and Sometimes Hate) Story in Maps by 75 New Yorkers* (Cooper 2013).

8.5   Ethical Reasoning: The Ethics of Mapping

Maps are abstractions, typically erasing the details of people's actual lives. They also have been used as instruments of persuasion, domination, and oppression by more-powerful groups over vulnerable groups. Under what conditions can—and should—ethical ethnographic mapping take place? Before you address this question, have a look at the table on the inside cover to remind yourself of key ethical principles.

CRITICAL THINKING

CHAPTER NINE

VISUALIZING

Many anthropologists incorporate some strategy of visual documentation into their fieldwork. Approaches can range from the creation of graphics, diagrams, maps, and illustrative drawings to photography or the production of film or video. The obvious advantage is to enable the fieldworker to record and produce fine-grained detail about the appearance of an event, activity, group, person, concept, process, or nonlinguistic forms of communication. Like written field notes, visual images can be useful to help jog a fieldworker's memory after the fieldwork is finished, and some might, of course, reach publication and dissemination as illustrations in a text. With the expansion of digital technologies and hypermedia, the possibilities for visual documentation and presentation have become accessible even to those anthropologists not trained formally in visual anthropology, a small sub-branch of cultural anthropology that is traditionally focused on documentary film production and, more recently, broadly defined visual cultures (media, arts, hypermedia) (Pink 2013).

Whatever recording device is utilized—a sketching pencil and pad, still camera, or video camera—the results can never be a direct inscription of reality because the fieldworker and the technological device itself filter and mediate reality in particular ways. Referring to the use of cameras in fieldwork, for example, the anthropologist Gregory Bateson once observed, "Of the things that happen, the camera is only going to record 1 percent anyway. . . . I want that 1 percent on the whole to tell" (Mead and Bateson 2002: 43). Bateson's point was that cameras—still and film—have limited fields of vision and can't be used at all times. He railed against the naive idea that you could simply place a camera on a tripod, push the record button, and make meaningful images for cultural analysis. He understood that the fieldworker needs to make intentional choices about what to record and how to record it, interacting with others in the process. Making pictures, in other words, is never a simple act of documentation and recording but an act of *creation* and *representation* that exists within and reflects particular *relationships*. As representations, visual data are subject to the social context—and the individual ethnographic eye and desire for communication—that shapes their production. This position is now widely accepted across anthropology (Banks and Morphy 1997).

Generally, anthropologists have three ways of approaching visual data, each of which carries distinctive considerations (adapted from Banks 1995):

- **Studying the visual representations of others.** Fieldworkers often collect and observe the creation of visual images or displays, such as photographs, films, drawings, paintings, sculptures, etc., that are produced by participants in the research. What interests the fieldworker is the image or the display's *content*—what does it mean and how is the image or display interpreted by those who make and use it?— and the *context*—how and why was it made, and by whom? In this mode, the fieldworker might conduct various kinds of interviews and participant observation to better understand content and context.

- **Self-created representations.** The motivation of fieldworkers who create photos, films, or illustrative drawings themselves is usually the desire to represent content and subject matter. But as noted above, it's just as important to pay attention to the context. Fieldworkers are social actors as well, and our values, perspectives, and relationships with others shape the kinds of images we produce. In an effort to recognize this point, some anthropological filmmakers have stepped in front of the camera to show their role in creating images, and anthropologists who create still images or sketches often write about the context in which they created the image.

- **Collaborative representations.** "Taking" a picture can be seen as an extractive act, generating concerns about unequal power relationships and who has control over the production and circulation of an image. Recognizing that there are politics in image making, many fieldworkers decide (or are pressured) to collaborate with research participants

KEY RESOURCE. This excerpt is from a dialogue that took place between Margaret Mead and Gregory Bateson about the uses of cameras in anthropology (Mead and Bateson 2002).

to create images—deciding with them what images to create and how they will be used, and sometimes jointly composing and creating the actual images themselves. Although fieldworkers still view their goals as research goals, some approach this kind of collaboration as a means of supporting those individuals and communities desiring to create respectful images of themselves.

It should be clear that in all these modes, visual documentation is not simply an act of recording, and seeing should not necessarily be believing. It also involves acts of judgment, framing, relationship building, and interpretation by a fieldworker.

Approaching the Visual

Like languages and text-based writing, visual images follow certain conventional patterns of **syntax** (arrangement and composition of elements) and **semantics** (how meaning is made) (Scott and Garner 2013). Each medium of visual representation—photography, filming, drawing, and others—carries its own syntactical and semantic rules for constructing messages.

Nevertheless, when approaching—or making—visual objects in any medium, it helps to know these basic patterns of visual communication:

Syntax	*Perspective*, or point of view. *Scale*, or the proportionality of objects in the image. *Angle of vision*, which affects perspective. *Lighting and shadow*, which emphasize or deemphasize something. *Framing*, or what's included and its arrangement. *Foregrounding and depth of field*, or what's in front and behind it. *Use of symbols*. If applicable, *motion*. How are these individual techniques used to capture and focus your attention?
Semantics	Who is the author and what is the author's purpose? Who is the intended audience? What values, perspectives, or histories are represented? How might different people interpret this image differently from you? What is omitted from the image?

KEY RESOURCE. The book *Visual Methods in Social Research* (Banks and Zeitlyn 2015) is a treasure trove of methodological advice and research strategies for working with visual materials.

FIELDWORK TIP

Cameras, both still and video, can sometimes disrupt social action and make people nervous and self-conscious. Anonymity can also be compromised. So don't try to "sneak" photos, since it can violate trust and protection of collaborators' identities. It's best to be open about image making, asking for permission to take photos, and to use the opportunity to create or deepen a social relationship. Offer to share copies of your photos.

Whether you are working with images already created, or creating your own, keep these ideas in mind—*and practice them*. Strong visual analysis is rooted in a practiced ability to use these analytical techniques, and intentional image making also draws on them. In the first exercise, the goal is to consider in more detail how, and what, photographs communicate.

9.1 Interpreting the "Truth" of a Photograph

CRITICAL THINKING

The well-known art critic John Berger and photographer Jean Mohr once wrote, "In itself the photograph cannot lie, but by the same token, it cannot tell the truth; or rather, the truth it does tell, the truth it can by itself defend, is a limited one" (Berger and Mohr 1982: 97). Find a photograph taken by someone else—either a physical photograph in your possession or a digital one that you find and print out—and tape it here. Write your thoughts about how the truth in this photograph "is a limited one."

_____

_____

_____

_____

_____

_____

_____

_____

_____

_____

_____

_____

_____

_____

_____

_____

_____

_____

_____

_____

_____

_____

_____

_____

_____

_____

_____

_____

_____

_____

_____

_____

_____

9.2   Grab a Flyer

COMMUNICATION • CRITICAL THINKING

Take a flyer being given out or hanging somewhere in your field site or campus. Fold it up, tape it here, and explain the context in which you found it and what it refers to, and do a close description of how it graphically represents its theme in the following ways:

Syntax:

_____

_____

_____

_____

_____

_____

_____

_____

_____

_____

_____

_____

_____

_____

_____

_____

_____

_____

_____

Semantics:

_____

_____

_____

_____

_____

_____

_____

_____

_____

_____

_____

_____

_____

_____

_____

_____

_____

_____

_____

_____

_____

_____

_____

_____

_____

_____

_____

FIELDWORK TIP

In Addition to the Flyer . . . You can do a version of this exercise with visual objects other than a flyer. Other possibilities include:

- an object in a museum display
- an object in a commercial environment, such as a grocery store or specialty shop
- a photo display
- an advertisement
- a tattoo parlor display of images

The specific details of syntax and semantics will likely differ across these settings.

9.3 Two Photographs, Two Different Approaches

In this exercise you will make two different photographs, one self-created and the other collaborative. Grab your smartphone or camera and approach somebody *you don't know* doing something. Introduce yourself to that person, ask his or her permission to take a photo, and explain what your goal is. For your first photograph, take it yourself, taking into consideration both the syntactical and semantic dimensions of your photograph. Find another person and approach him or her in the same way, but this time let the individual make suggestions about how to compose the photograph—ask what you should photograph about him or her and how she or he would like you to do it. Print out the two photos and tape them here. Write an explanation of the process you used in each, describe in writing the key details of the photo, and assess the differences between the two approaches to photography.

NETWORKING • COMMUNICATION • LISTENING • WORKING WITH DIFFERENCE

9.4   Drawing as Ethnographic Inquiry

Many anthropologists use their field journals to draw things and sketch scenes, although drawing on the whole has not played a major role in disciplinary communication. But connecting creativity and practice with fieldwork through drawing can help generate new kinds of understanding and expressive possibilities (Ingold 2011, Taussig 2011). It can also create new or collaborative relationships with people whose lives you are observing and asking about, because sketching a scene (instead of taking a picture of one with a camera, say) means you stick around longer, creating opportunities for informal interactions. Draw or sketch a picture or scene here about a situation, event, or comment that came up during an interview or observation.

COMMUNICATION • ACCURACY AND ATTENTION TO DETAIL

Reflection: How does sketching or drawing help or hinder your access and insight into your subject?

CRITICAL THINKING

_____

_____

_____

_____

_____

_____

_____

_____

_____

_____

_____

_____

_____

_____

_____

_____

_____

_____

_____

_____

_____

KEY RESOURCES. Although they are not methodology or how-to books, both Tim Ingold's edited book _Redrawing Anthropology: Materials, Movements, Lines_ (Ingold 2011) and Michael Taussig's _I Swear I Saw This: Drawings in Fieldwork Notebooks, Namely My Own_ (Taussig 2011) explore the possibilities drawing offers for cultivating anthropological insight.

9.5   Diagram It!

Another graphical approach to anthropology is to make a diagram, a symbolic representation in the form of a chart, graphic, or schematic, about something. Kinship charts, which diagram family relationships, come to mind. Create a diagram about a social dynamic, relationship, or process you have observed in your fieldwork or daily life. Give some thought and be intentional about what form for your diagram works best. If nothing comes to mind, familiarize yourself with the conventions and symbols of kinship charts (presented in practically any introduction-to-anthropology book) and create a kinship chart of a friend.

NETWORKING • COMMUNICATION • ACCURACY AND ATTENTION TO DETAIL

9.6   Ethical Reasoning: The Ethics of Visual Culture

It is often said that seeing is an ethical act. There are two dimensions to this, one being how the production of images might influence the moral perspectives and ethical behaviors of others, and the other being how we ethically respond to images. Can you think of or describe an image you recently saw that created distance or empathy? If not, go find one and describe it here. What syntactical and semantic techniques did it use to achieve the effect? How might that image shape an ethical response to the situation? Do you have an ethical responsibility to respond to an image that is deliberately manipulative?

_____

_____

_____

_____

_____

_____

_____

_____

_____

_____

_____

_____

_____

_____

_____

_____

CHAPTER TEN

EXPERIENCING

Every day we learn things about the world around us from direct experiential involvement in it. Much of that learning is focused on practical matters when getting things done. We also learn about the people around us by being experientially involved with them, and sometimes our experiences with others can help us learn about ourselves, such as when we recognize ourselves reacting in a new or unexpected way to something someone has done. A lot of this learning is subtle, expressing itself through embodied senses of pleasure, stress, or some other physical or emotional reaction.

We tend not to keep formal track of the many things we learn from direct experience. But fieldworkers do, or at least try to, recognizing that direct experiential and embodied involvement can contribute to the creation of important anthropological insights and knowledge. "Experience" is central to the anthropological research technique of "participation," but they are not equivalent concepts. Participation refers to a deliberate decision made by an outsider to "join in" some kind of action, bracketed perhaps by a beginning and an end to the joining in. Experience is what the active, conscious, feeling, and reflecting self undergoes during and beyond that action (Turner and Bruner

KEY RESOURCE. This basic fact, that we can know only our own experience, hasn't stopped anthropologists from ethnographic research on cross-cultural variations in experience and selfhood. A classic primer on the "anthropology of experience" is Victor Turner and Edward Bruner's edited book *The Anthropology of Experience* (Turner and Bruner 1986).

1986). While we can observe the participation of others and perhaps interpret what they are experiencing from their outward expressions, in the end we can really know only our own individual experiences.

Until relatively recently, anthropologists tended to edit out personal field-work experiences from published texts. This is partly because Western academic culture artificially separates "knowing" from "feeling" (Rosaldo 1989, Hovland 2007). Fieldwork is also an untidy personal experience that doesn't necessarily fit neatly into an analytical narrative about social life in a community. Fieldwork typically happens in fits and starts and engenders feelings of apprehension, anxiety, loneliness, homesickness, frustration, vulnerability, and powerlessness, not to mention joy, exhilaration, and camaraderie . . . all of which might be experienced in the course of a single day. Fieldwork can also be a transformative life experience, creating a new sense of self in the field-worker. A self-reflexive fieldworker understands that whatever personal feelings and experiences he or she has can color and shape what gets written into field notes, and will often jot down emotional or reflective reactions to situations in the notes themselves. These jottings can help the "future self" reading the notes contextualize the content and tone of the field notes better, even drawing attention to the emotional tenor of the event or setting for others who were present.

Other fieldworkers choose a strategy of formally separating out their "field notes," where they record data, from a personal diary or journal where they process their experiences, vent the joys and frustrations of their day, stew over mistakes they might have made, and reflect on relationships with participants in the research. With critical estrangement—and usually some time and emotional distance—these raw writings can become useful field notes themselves, in which the future self might pick up on social patterns or dynamics in which he or she was directly involved that were unapparent or hazy at the time of fieldwork. The opportunity here lies in recognizing oneself as a subject

KEY RESOURCE. Malinowski's Diary. Although he is known for emphasizing an emotionally distant writing style in his publications, Bronislaw Malinowski kept a diary while conducting fieldwork that is full of frustrations, uncertainties, and longings (Malinowski 1989). Some of what he said has provoked controversy, but his diaries offer an important demonstration that observing and interviewing others is not value-free or separable from explorations of the self. In subsequent years, numerous anthropologists have published diaries and personal reflections on the ups, downs, and epiphanies of fieldwork.

involved in systematic social relations that are pushing, pulling, and placing expectations on ethnographer and native alike. In the first exercise, you have a chance to try out the kind of journaling referred to here.

DIRECTED LEARNING • CRITICAL THINKING

10.1 Reflective Journaling

In fieldwork, reflective journaling offers a means to review and reflect on personal experience. It's an open-ended form of writing with infinite prompts and no rules, except being honest with yourself. Write here about a key event or experience you had while doing one of the exercises in this book or other fieldwork. If you need a prompt, think of a situation that energized you (or, alternatively, felt draining to you). Write about what occurred or was experienced, who else was involved, how you can explain or make sense of it, and what might have been learned from the experience.

_____

_____

_____

_____

_____

_____

_____

_____

_____

_____

_____

_____

_____

_____

_____

_____

_____

_____

_____

_____

_____

_____

_____

_____

_____

_____

_____

_____

_____

_____

_____

_____

_____

_____

_____

_____

_____

10.2   Serendipity, Mistakes, and Unexpected Occurrences

DIRECTED LEARNING

Part of being a good fieldworker is being open to learning from mistakes, unexpected situations, chance occurrences, and fluky situations, because these can reveal relationships, issues, or dynamics we hadn't yet recognized. But it takes a certain kind of self-consciousness and critical estrangement when we are directly involved in these situations to make anthropological sense of them. Think about a mistake you made, a serendipitous occasion, a strange coincidence, or a chance occurrence, either in your fieldwork or in your daily life. What questions does it raise for you? Are there any anthropological insights that could be derived from it?

CRITICAL THINKING

Autoethnography

The genre of research and writing called **autoethnography** combines ethnographic fieldwork in a community with the fieldworker's autobiography, using personal experiences and storytelling to systematically explore and analyze dimensions of cultural experience (Ellis et al. 2011). It embraces the notion that fieldwork cannot be done from a neutral or objective stance, and acknowledges that the fieldworker's subjectivity, emotions, and relationships shape the knowledge created. One of its central goals is to use personal stories to sensitize readers to issues of identity politics, to demonstrate diverse assumptions about the world, and to deepen empathy for people who are different from us (Ellis and Bochner 2000).

KEY RESOURCES. Further Background on Autoethnography.
There are numerous methodological guides that explain autoethnographic approaches and how-to's in more detail. See *Autoethnography as Method* (Chang 2008) and *Auto/Ethnography: Rewriting the Self and the Social* (Reed-Danahay 1997). Ruth Behar's *The Vulnerable Observer: Anthropology That Breaks Your Heart* (Behar 1997) is an excellent example of an autoethnographic text.

Autoethnography is both process and product, a method of research *and* a written outcome. Autoethnographers conduct participant observation in a community as any other fieldworker does, but they are especially attentive to any personal epiphanies, special insights, or transformations in identity made possible by their involvement in a social community and its culture. Many of these epiphanies are made in hindsight and are written about retrospectively but can provoke new periods of fieldwork exploring how cultural insiders have also experienced similar epiphanies or transformations in their own identities. While autoethnography is story driven, what differentiates it from "just" anybody else's personal story is that it also draws on scholarly literature and fieldwork to analyze how cultural processes shape the identity and experience of cultural insiders and outsiders.

10.3	**Contemplating an Autoethnographic Project**

DIRECTED LEARNING • ADAPTABILITY

Give some thought to how you would design an autoethnographic research project on the experience of schooling at the university level. On the basis of all you are learning here about fieldwork, what would be your major research strategies?

_____

_____

_____

_____

_____

_____

_____

_____

_____

_____

_____

_____

_____

_____

_____

_____

_____

_____

_____

_____

_____

WORKING WITH DIFFERENCE • CRITICAL THINKING

10.4 Ethical Reasoning: Autoethnography and Relational Ethics

Concerns about relational ethics are heightened for autoethnographers because they often write narratives that communicate stories about people with whom they are intimate—close friends, neighbors, children, and so on. Because those stories might make those intimates uncomfortable or put them at risk of unflattering portrayals, autoethnographers often share what they have written with those individuals before publishing it to get their responses to it and maintain trusting relationships. What kinds of opportunities and complications do you think sharing such writings could generate for the anthropologist?

COMMUNICATION • CRITICAL THINKING

_____

_____

_____

Space for Extra Notes

CHAPTER ELEVEN

GOING DIGITAL

Since the start of the 21st century, an increasing number of anthropologists have "gone digital," conducting fieldwork in online communities, social media, and virtual worlds. Employing the discipline's traditional holistic, comparative, and relativistic perspectives, they have found that online worlds and social relationships are as real, diverse, dynamic, ambiguous, and complicated as those in any "offline" social community. At the same time, the fact that the fieldworker dwells online for substantial periods, interacting in technologically mediated environments with people who are (potentially) living in geographically dispersed areas, presents a distinct set of opportunities and challenges, shaped by factors such as the following:

- **The technological specificities of online platforms**. Digital platforms enable and limit communication and social interaction in highly specific ways. For example, a social-media platform such as Twitter broadcasts messages of 140 words, while in a virtual world such as Second Life, participants literally construct, dwell, socialize, and even make money in the online world they create.

- **Complex intersections of global and local**. The scale of many Internet platforms is transnational and their participants are geographically dispersed, yet those participants will also filter and interact with the Internet and each other through culturally specific lenses and meanings and localized social networks.

- **Managing social identities online**. Online environments allow for the construction, performance, and management of new kinds of identities, which can heighten questions of anonymity, trust, and deception. Fieldworkers do not navigate these issues in isolation; most online communities have to work through these issues as well, creating opportunities for the fieldworker to study these processes up close.

- **The ephemeral nature of online social relationships**. Although plenty of online communities exist with relatively stable participants and specific norms, many social activities and relationships online are fleeting, transient, and difficult to pin down.

- **Fluidity and interdependency between offline and online worlds**. The "virtual world" of the Internet is not growing away from the "real world." Internet spaces are embedded within, and interdependent with, offline relationships. Online interactions may be one "node" in a social network that spans multiple digital platforms and offline social processes, gatherings, and institutions. Fieldwork may involve moving between these nodes, conducting interviews and participant observation in all of them.

- **Connectivity, access to equipment, and technical proficiency**. For a digital fieldworker, having the devices and developing the technical know-how to participate in digital worlds are critical. At the same time, it is important for the fieldworker to recognize that many people around the world do not have access to these things—because of poverty, lack of connectivity, and other reasons—which means that it is problematic to make generalizations about something such as the impact of the Internet on social relations made from a small slice of globally privileged Internet users.

- **Electronic data collection**. In addition to interviews and participant observation both online and offline, digital fieldworkers can gather data utilizing Internet archives and by capturing chatlogs (logs from chat rooms or sidebar chats), screenshots, video, and audio. In projects involving social media, where updates are constant, managing information overload with various kinds of filtering and search tools is important.

Given these dynamics, as well as the fact that many platforms have millions of participants, it can be daunting to define the scope and nature of the "community" under study. Digital fieldworkers will thus often get involved in

---

KEY RESOURCES. This list derives from several sources that offer useful background on digital anthropology, including Miller and Slater 2000, Boellstorff 2008, and Horst and Miller 2012.

👍 **KEY RESOURCE. Resources for Digital Field Methods**. Two books published since 2010 examine digital ethnography methods in detail: *Ethnography and Virtual Worlds: A Handbook of Method* (Boellstorff et al. 2012) and *Digital Ethnography: Principles and Practice* (Pink et al. 2015).

somewhat bounded subgroups organized around the intensive use of social media or participation in virtual worlds. These might include guilds in multiplayer gaming platforms such as World of Warcraft, interest groups or social networks on Facebook, communities of practice in a virtual world such as Second Life, "cyberactivist" or protest movements using Twitter, hackers in corners of the "Dark Web," and so on. They might focus on users from a particular geographic area, looking for opportunities to identify crossings between online and offline worlds. Or they can choose a theme of traditional anthropological interest—such as law and order, social inequality, kinship relations, or sexual identities—and examine how these themes are expressed and enacted in a specific digital setting. Whatever the project, the open-ended nature of fieldwork encourages the fieldworker to follow individuals as they move across, within, and beyond the online communities and activities in which they are involved.

Digital fieldwork is still in its infancy, but as the following exercises demonstrate, the range of possible projects is wide.

11. 1   Approaching Fieldwork in a Virtual World

Choose a virtual world (also known as a Massively Multiplayer Online World) such as Second Life, Active World, or Small Worlds, or a multiplayer game such as World of Warcraft. Examine the entry portals and conditions for joining and participating. Also, use a web search engine to find a site or two focused on advice for new players/residents of your chosen world or game. Jot down here the responses to these questions: What are the rules and social norms involved in being active in this world? Are there particular processes of enculturation (initiation and socialization) for newcomers? If you have interest or time, or if your course allows it, join the world and get to know it. Design a fieldwork project studying some dimension of this world. Make a list here of possible project ideas.

DIRECTED LEARNING • CURIOSITY

ADAPTABILITY

KEY RESOURCE. Ethnographies of Virtual Worlds. The books *Coming of Age in Second Life* (Boellstorff 2008) and *My Life as a Night Elf Priest: An Anthropological Account of World of Warcraft* (Nardi 2010), both early ethnographic accounts of virtual worlds, explain their research strategies in detail.

Ethnography and Social Media

Social networking sites such as Facebook, Twitter, YouTube, Instagram, Snapchat, and others have gained millions of followers, affecting how friends, family, lovers, and antagonists interact with each other. They have had consequential effects on privacy, anonymity, fame, community, politics, and work. But there is a lot of hype, often produced by social-media companies themselves, about the transformative effects of social media on people's lives, and ethnographic fieldwork can serve as a grounded and realistic check on that hype. In his essay "Fifteen Theses on What Facebook Might Be," anthropologist Daniel Miller, in his *Tales from Facebook* (Miller 2011: 165), observes that it is necessary to start by appreciating "that each and every individual was quite literally a social networking site long before Facebook existed." In other words, social media has not "consumed" people so much as people have consumed it, integrating it into their social networks as one of multiple communication tools, albeit with specific technological limitations and possibilities, that they use to interact with each other. Indeed, one of Miller's 15 theses on Facebook is that social media has not really expanded people's social networks, but *intensified* them. A key ethnographic task of digital fieldwork in social media is to relativize and contextualize how, why, and for what people use a particular social-media platform, the meanings they make of their activities and relationships with it, and how their activities in social media exist interdependently (or not) with offline lives.

11.2 Fieldwork on Facebook

Assess how people interact on Facebook by studying wall posts (or, if you don't have Facebook, its public posts). List here the focus of three wall posts. Describe how an individual presents him or herself, how visitors respond to it, and how the individual responds back. Can you characterize the kinds of themes, issues, and debates that go back and forth in wall posts? Are there certain implicit notions about how one should interact through wall posts?

DIRECTED LEARNING • CURIOSITY

_____

_____

_____

_____

Reflection: What could you learn about how people interact with each other in social networking by focusing on wall posts alone? What other aspects of Facebook could you study to better understand social relationships in this digital platform?

_____

_____

_____

_____

_____

_____

_____

_____

_____

_____

_____

_____

_____

_____

_____

_____

_____

_____

_____

_____

_____

_____

KEY RESOURCE. *Tales from Facebook* (Miller 2011) is a good starting point for understanding how to approach social-networking sites anthropologically. There you can also review Miller's 14 other "theses on what Facebook might be."

11.3   #Twitterography

Some digital fieldworkers have turned to Twitter to study, for example, cyberactivism where Twitter is used as an instantaneous news tool and social-organizing platform, or to track the use and shifting meanings of certain kinds of words and terms. Twitter has limits: it has a relatively small number of users to begin with, its search function is imprecise, tweets are often incomplete, and interactions are ephemeral (Postill and Pink 2012). But one technique, which you can try out here, is to "follow" a set number of users (10–20) and track their tweets (noting the topic and reactions to it) as well as their retweets over a period of several days. Be intentional about why you chose those users and explain your rationale here. What kinds of "conversations" or debates occur? What are the relative "rhythms" (frequency and intensity) of Twitter activity and how can you explain the changes in rhythm?

DIRECTED LEARNING • CURIOSITY • ADAPTABILITY

DIRECTED LEARNING • CURIOSITY • ADAPTABILITY • CRITICAL THINKING

11.4 | What's New in Social Media?

New social-media apps and sites emerge all the time. Some of these newcomers (relative to Facebook, at least), such as Instagram, Yik-Yak, and Snapchat, have gained widespread followings, especially among college students. Identify a new form of social media that you know about and write a plan here for how you would study its adoption or uses ethnographically. If you would like to actually do some interviews around the subject, identify a number of people in your social networks involved in the site and ask them: How, why, and under what circumstances do individuals choose to move from one platform to another? What do they find appealing—and limiting—about this platform compared to others they know? How does the new site affect their relationship with social media? Write your notes here.

Blogging Fieldwork

Some researchers write blogs while they are doing fieldwork. Fieldwork can be a slow process that comes in fits and starts, with episodes of intensity followed by periods of not feeling like much is happening. So it doesn't necessarily align well with the immediate feedback and sound-bite communication style of the Web. Yet, some fieldworkers have overcome these tensions by creating a blog where they write regular or semiregular reflective postings on what they are learning in the fieldwork. While these postings may sometimes carry "raw field notes," they are typically a step or two removed from those notes and instead describe emerging patterns, insights, or analyses of themes that are popping up in their work.

Another approach to fieldwork and blogging is to combine the two more intensively, such as with "live fieldnoting" (Wang 2012). Similar to "liveblogging" (continuously covering an ongoing event by using Twitter or a blogging tool), live field noting combines writing field notes and picture taking and "live" posting to Instagram. The method involves using a smartphone to take pictures during participant observation or interviews, creating a photo collection on Instagram, and adding captions of raw notes, explanations, observations, descriptions, and whatever else either during or right after a fieldwork

> 👍 **KEY RESOURCES. "Live Fieldnoting" and Other "Ethnography Matters."** The collaboratively produced blog *Ethnography Matters* (http://ethnographymatters.net) is a forum for discussing issues in ethnographic methods, often digital ones. It is where, for example, you can find Tricia Wang's essay explaining live field noting: "Writing Live Fieldnotes: Towards a More Open Ethnography" (Wang 2012).

event. Since the images are posted to the Web, it is especially important that participants understand this and give consent for their images to be online.

11.5 Ethical Reasoning: Digital-Fieldwork Ethics

COMMUNICATION • CRITICAL THINKING

Conducting fieldwork in digital environments raises ethical concerns much as fieldwork in any social community does, but it can complicate or intensify certain dynamics and dilemmas. For example, privacy protections and anonymity can be difficult to ensure since many of the data that digital fieldworkers collect is textual and searchable by others. Another concern is the ability digital fieldworkers have to eavesdrop or "lurk" online without being noticed by others, not informing them that research is happening and that they have the right to give their informed consent. Consider these questions:

How do you think a digital fieldworker can or should anonymize textual data collected online?

_____

_____

_____

_____

How do you think a digital fieldworker can and should gain informed consent online? Think about how the dynamics of receiving informed consent might differ between fieldwork on a social-networking site and in a virtual world.

_____

_____

_____

_____

Examine the AAA ethical principles table, which does not explic-
itly address digital-fieldwork ethics. Do you think it should? If you
had to suggest new ethical principles for digital fieldworkers to
add to this table, what would they be?

_____

_____

_____

_____

Space for Extra Notes

Space for Extra Notes

PART III

WORKING WITH FIELDWORK DATA

Fieldwork projects are unruly experiences that produce a lot of data, most of which appears, on the surface at least, to be disconnected, fragmented, and full of loose ends. Although knowing "how much fieldwork is enough" is never a straightforward matter, with time, focus, energy, and resourcefulness most fieldworkers produce notebooks full of snippets, sketches, and extended descriptions of varying quality, length, and style; binders packed with printed interview transcripts; irregularly sized collections of reports, newspaper articles, etc.; computer files of field notes and digital voice or video recordings; and envelopes spilling out with visual materials, slips of paper, index cards, Post-its, and other random fragments. Keeping a handle on all this material can be challenging, if, like me, you have a touch of disorganization about you.

But knowing *what* to do with all those data can be even more daunting. Like fieldwork itself, working with field notes is a directed learning process with emergent, creative, and unpredictable qualities, and there are no simple formulas for proceeding. Nevertheless, there are a number of distinct practices that can make this process manageable, enriching, and even exhilarating. The purpose of this last section is to introduce you to the range of the practices involved in processing and analyzing field notes and then crafting an ethnographic account.

CHAPTER TWELVE

PROCESSING FIELD NOTES

Processing field notes requires stepping back from the discipline of writing them and beginning to use them for their purpose and potential as descriptive and sense-making documents. At various points during a fieldwork project, it is important to take stock of and work with the notes you have, although the goals, priorities, and approaches toward working with field notes will shift over time.

It Begins during Fieldwork . . .

Experienced fieldworkers know that beginning to work with their data shouldn't wait until active fieldwork is over. Processing notes may mean periodically organizing and cleaning them up so they are legible and retrievable later. But there is also a critical research design element to it. While in the midst of fieldwork, it is important to begin sifting through the accumulating data, reading for emergent threads, patterns, regularities, and connections. Many fieldworkers write data memos (see below) to explore these things. These reading-and-writing processes should progressively focus and strategically direct the research, as well as identify any gaps or misunderstandings that can be clarified with targeted interviews, participant-observation, and other techniques. Interpretation and analysis is thus not a distinct stage of the research process but is organically tied to the process of data collection itself.

129

Another time is when active fieldwork is coming to a close. It sometimes seems like fieldwork could go on indefinitely—there is always more to learn, more people to hear from, more events to attend. Although the difficulties of managing one's identity as an insider-outsider can be exhausting over time, usually the impetus to end active fieldwork is some external factor: a research paper deadline is looming, funding runs out, or family or career advancement is calling. As active fieldwork is ending, it is especially important to assess your confidence—or lack of confidence—in your notes. By now, certain general themes in the research stand out. As best as you can tell, is your data about those themes *reliable*? Did you triangulate and confirm details of important stories, events, or relationships from multiple perspectives? Are you still missing key perspectives that would deepen your understanding of a particular story or situation? You still have a chance to follow up to clarify those details.

. . . and It Ramps Up after the Fieldwork Is Over

After ending active fieldwork, it is possible to approach field notes and everything else you collected as a whole data set. In this phase—"deskwork" as opposed to "fieldwork" (Marcus 1980)—you will carefully read through the whole corpus, multiple times, looking for any regular, surprising, or puzzling patterns, raising any questions that emerge, and formulating analytical concepts to apply to the data. You should strive to approach your field notes as if they were written by a stranger, although this is admittedly difficult because of the personal relationships and experiences reflected in the notes (Emerson et al. 2011).

These efforts start by **coding** the notes, usually defined as successively condensing relevant data into categories and concepts, and then making analytic connections between those categories and the data. Here you take all those fragments of data and begin identifying any systematic patterns and connections in and across them. Coding involves multiple passes through the data, including (adapted and modified from Emerson et al. 2011) the following:

- **Open coding**. The first pass through the data involves a chronological line-by-line read from the earliest notes to those made last. As you locate *any* theme, issue, or pattern—the goal being to be open to any analytic possibilities—you tag it with a "code," a key word or several-worded label, in the margins or on another piece of paper. The code simultaneously provides a conceptual marker and flags it in the data. Open coding is a creative, interpretive process, and different ethnographers might code the same set of notes differently, given differences in background, theoretical perspective, and other factors. Open

✱ Democracy, privatization, social divisions.

community. It wouldn't work b.c of this - people would be fighting too much b/w themselves within the school - different people would want power within the board.

"fight" (what kind?)   *(Carlos: quiet.*

C: The problem is, not everybody can send their kids to a private school. Only the rich could do it...

← Circumscribing public s.

A: (aggressively) what about grants?

C: ... the poor kids won't be able to go, but the rich will be able to. And that means that the child of the poor will always continue to be working for the child of the rich man. I can't send my kids to a private school...

← class (rich v. poor)

A: Yes, but it would make a better high school.

F: Yes, there's no doubt. I agree with you on that, Amy. And I think that's fine that there should be a private high school so that there's a good education here in the zone. But there needs to be a public high school always, to provide opportunities for those who can't pay to go the private school. This is a democratic country, and people can do what they want - if they want a private school, they can make one. This is why other countries have civil wars, b.c the rich people control all the poor people. The other thing is that not every student who is in a school is going to be prevented from doing well, even if the teachers are bad. Look at me. I never had a supervision, I never got suspended. I was respectful, and I definitely had my run-ins with teachers. But this never held me back - I did my work and I graduate fine. So I don't think that just b/c its a public h.s. the student is going to not learn...

problem w/ privatization invokes "democracy" theme of war individualism??

Amy went to the desk for a second.

T: Grants have limits - not all students get them..

A: I didn't mean to say that there should be no public schools...

Created zone + dialogue (Amy)

F: Of course not. I don't have any problems with schools like the Adventist School here. Or the Centro Pedagogico. More power to them if they want to educate their kids. This is a democratic country. The thing it would do is create social groups here.

democracy = do what you want... "social groups" / hoteleros

A: What do you mean by social groups? Are there any?

F: Of course there are... Look at the hoteleros. They make up a social group. They have their meetings where they talk about their businesses. How would I, who don't own a hotel, become part of that group? They wouldn't even let me probably. I have nothing to say to them...

→ they exclude him. he excludes them

A: But you say there are groups - like what?

F: I can't think of any others, really, right now. But think about these little groups ('grupillos') that are around. The hoteleros are one of these grupillos. They think they are separate from the rest of the people here. You know that I work with the police as a backup here - it makes me laugh to think about it. The other saturday we got a call that Geovanny Arguedas was trashing the Orquideas - we go there, and he had overturned tables, broken glass, and he was yelling 'I'm Geovanny Arguedas, owner of Sapo Dorado! I'm owner of the Sapo! I'm Geovanny Arguedas!' It was sad, really. They got him, and told him to quit - they didn't throw him in jail - they just told him to leave. He said he could drive, so they let him go under his own cognizance. He wasn't even drunk really...

"grupillos"
→ behaviors of entitled hoteleros.

A: Oh my...

F: He had nothing before Hanna. I remember, b/c we used to hang out a lot. The beer truck would come, and he wouldn't have a dime towards buying a beer, and he'd borrow... He was always broke. Hanna made that hotel what it is - it's her money. She's a classy woman.

'themselves' hoteleros was one of when... not now...

A: But it was his land...

F: Yeah, he built the club on his dad's land.

C: There are two types of drunks here. The ones who, like me, drink 4 beers, and then leave - they do it to have fun or relax. Then there's the other, who drinks until he can barely stand. [he then left]

"two types of drunks"
← Carlos backs off...

A: Is it true that Geovanny is screwing around?

F: What a gossip! I know who you're thinking about, the doctora, but she's more of a bicho than he is... There's no doubt that he's a dog. I remember when he stole that

check on conversation

Privatization & benefits "grupillos" / hoteleros

FIGURE 12.1 **Open-Coded Notes.** This page, one of several thousand from my field notes on environmentalism in rural Costa Rica for my dissertation and first book (Vivanco 2006), was open coded. The notes themselves were from a conversation between workers at a community-run cloud forest preserve. Coding it helped me identify and begin unpacking ongoing tensions among workers about a proposal to privatize the preserve. Key codes on this page were "democracy," "privatization," "grupillos / social groupings," and "hoteleros" (hotel owners), and I eventually wrote about the complex relationships between these categories.

coding should not rely on preestablished categories—the goal is to open up new ideas and lines of inquiry, helping you "see" things you may not have seen before (figure 12.1).

- **Selective coding**. In the second pass, the focus is on reviewing those preliminary codes, to identify any core themes, key concepts, or sub-codes in them. This is done by looking for frequencies, linkages, and comparisons between the codes. Once key concepts and themes are identified—and they can be tentative—one now goes back to the data and "tests" these new core themes by sorting out sections and examples that exhibit or seem to diverge from them. Selective codes might be written in the margins as well—though in a different color than the initial code to distinguish them—or on separate paper.
- **Focused coding**. In the third pass, the core themes and key concepts identified in selective coding now guide yet another read-through, in this case a very close reading. The goals now are to use those themes to connect new data that didn't previously appear connected and to identify differences and variations in the data related to the core themes, as well as the conditions under which those differences and variations occurred.

Coding can be slow, painstaking work, and it is not uncommon to identify gaps in knowledge, enough to (perhaps) motivate a focused and discrete return to active fieldwork. But it can also be exhilarating when previously unrecognized themes appear to jump out of the data. This process is not as simple as "discovering" something meaningful in the data, however, because the fieldworker's assumptions, theoretical orientations, and experiences influence what in the data appears meaningful. In the following exercise, you can try out a short coding activity. Try to be aware of where your own assumptions may be bringing certain issues to the fore.

FIELDWORK TIP

Computer-Aided Coding. Coding can be aided by widely available qualitative coding software such as Atlas.ti, Ethnograph, or HyperResearch, for which many universities have site licenses. Field notes are entered into a database, and codes still need to be created and linked to the data. What the software enables is rapid retrieval of coded data segments and tools that, for example, show code frequency in the data. Not all anthropologists use these programs, but they can be useful where there is a huge amount of data, or data collected by multiple people. Word-processing applications such as Word also have the ability to search for key words in a lot of data.

Working with field notes is a sense-making exercise. As Emerson et al. 1995 observes, "The analysis of fieldnotes is not just a matter of finding what the data contain. Rather, the ethnographer selects out some incidents and events, gives them priority, and comes to understand them in relationship to others" (p. 168).

12.1 Code Red!

DIRECTED LEARNING • CRITICAL THINKING

Part 1: Open-code this small selection of field notes drawn from my fieldwork on the politics and culture of urban bicycle use in Bogotá, Colombia. These notes were taken during and immediately after my participation in an organized group bike ride of several hundred people in the streets of Bogotá to promote environmental awareness. Grab a red pen (a good color for coding since it jumps out on the paper) and write your codes in the margin. While you won't have any direct experience or head notes to bring to this, if you read carefully you should be able to identify themes, issues, patterns, and questions.

> *Organizers told riders to meet at five points around the city (three in north of city, one in center, and one in south) at 3:30 and the five separate groups would converge at Parque Simon Bolivar for a "ciclopaseo nocturno" (night bike ride) in the park, and then a rock concert at Salitre Plaza Mall. I went to the central / Parque Nacional meet-up, arrived around 3:45. 15 or so people were standing around in 3 small groups. The Pedalea Bogotá representatives (mayor's office bike program) were one group I recognized and I greeted them. DM, the city's unofficial cycling photographer, approached me; he was registering people for the ride, asking them to fill out cards for a raffle (and collecting emails for later blasts).*
>
> *The little cliques forming here were different groups of friends/ members of the same colectivos (organized bike groups), some came together and others independently, but nobody was especially interested in crossing those lines between colectivos. RS, the city councilor and environmentalist leader, showed up w/ his wife, who works with the environmental group (Bogotá*

Basura Cero—Zero Trash Bogotá) that organized this event. This got some attention among the gathered groups.

Over the next hour people would trickle in, some arriving in groups of three or four, clearly having ridden together from some other gathering point. The BiciPachanga ("Bike Party") group showed up suddenly (it's now 4:30 or so), with two long cargo bikes and wearing costumes, J. on a fixie he was doing tricks on, CR on a tricycle with flags that had imprinted Bici-Pachanga and two large speakers on the back truck bed, blaring out techno-cumbia, Latin house, and rap music. It was electrifying and everybody's attention immediately shifted to them when they arrived. A few of us gravitated over to look at the unusual bikes.

Overhearing people, themes of conversation were often around bikes—where someone got something like an accessory, what it cost, etc. People taking pics of each other. RS was tweeting about the gathering and impending ride.

A guy asked me for my pen to fill out his raffle card, and when he did I complimented him on his bike, which was an old bike and decked out with recycled materials. "We have another rusted one over there" he pointed. He gave me his business card—the name of his business—"Los Años de Upa"—which finds and sells old bikes and bike parts. I asked significance of the name. He said it was a common Colombian expression "ese es de los años de upa" which means that something is really old.

Police starting showing up—auxiliaries (junior officers) on bicycle. One of the guys of Bogotá Pedalea eventually got everyone together, using the microphone of BiciPachanga when it was clear his voice wouldn't carry over the crowd of now maybe 60 (mostly young twenty-somethings; lots of mountain bikes, fixies; gender composition was probably ½ men).

"I'm ML and so that we have security for optimal control, I want to talk about how we will ride to Parque Nacional. We will have police escort. We will ride all together. We will respect traffic laws. We will be always united as a group." We slowly left, people falling into a long line, some riding side by side.

About five minutes in to the ride we stopped in the middle of the road, blocking automobiles following, and shouts began of "send BiciPachanga to the front!" They filtered to the front, music blaring. Lots of enthusiastic reactions form the riders.

Part 2: Go back and choose one of the observation or interview exercises you did earlier in this book and open-code it. Write which exercise you coded: _____ . Reflect here on any challenges or revelations about coding you had while doing it.

_____

_____

_____

_____

_____

_____

_____

_____

_____

_____

_____

Creating Research Memos

Another common mode of processing field notes, which can build on the coding process, is creating research memos. A research memo is a hybrid of note taking, reflective synthesis, and analytical writing. It is a deliberately free-form and open-ended memo to yourself, and there are no particular rules about length or style. Its importance lies as much in *process* as *product*, the goal being to get you thinking about and synthesizing data and key concepts. There are several different kinds of memos:

Data memo	Describes a rich or suggestive situation, vignette, or scenario, drawn from field notes and other collected data. Quotations from the data are especially important sources of evidence and illustration; descriptions of place, setting, individuals taking action, etc., are important as well. There is generally some reflection on how the data were gathered, their reliability, and any questions raised by the data. Often written during active fieldwork.
Analytical memo	Explores a particular set of core themes or key concepts in detail. Typically written after coding is completed, and drawing on field notes, it could involve explaining why a particular perspective or action might be reasonable within a specific context, as well as connections to other data points or theoretical observations drawn from relevant literature. It might focus on specific tensions, contradictions, paradoxes, complexities, and controversies identified in the data, seeking to draw those out through analysis, by exploring such questions as: What are the underlying patterns characterizing/shaping the phenomenon under study? What are some possible reasons for these things?
Graphic or diagram memo	Focuses on the creation of a visual graphic—a drawing, map, illustrative diagram, etc.—that synthesizes various data points drawn from field notes, or draws out concepts for analysis.

12.2   Create a Research Memo

In this exercise, create one of the types of memos described above, especially if you have been conducting a semester-long research project. Instead of creating it here, open a word-processing document, write it there, print it out, and staple it here.

- **Data memo**: Take a particular incident, situation, relationship, or quotation that you found out about in your fieldwork and write an expanded description of it.

- **Analytical memo**: Take one aspect of your data and write a memo making analytical connections between interviews, between interviews and observations, or between the data and something you have read. Alternatively, start with a core theme and expand on how that theme connects to literature you have been reading.

- **Graphic or diagram memo**: Draw a visual representation of a particular incident, situation, relationship, or quotation that you found out about from your fieldwork.

Reflection: Write here about any challenges or epiphanies you had while creating your memo.

_____

_____

_____

_____

_____

_____

Tools for Narrative Analysis

A common analytical task when processing field notes is interpreting stories and spoken accounts of connected events—in other words, **narratives**. Narratives typically have a plot and sequence, communicating an unfolding tale. Various types of interviews may produce narratives, such as structured or informal interviews, as well as oral-history interviews. Embedded in narratives are structured beliefs and understandings of everyday lived realities. Narrative conventions and patterns also usually reflect tacit cultural, gendered, class, or other notions about appropriate ways to tell a story. The goal of working with narratives is to search for and interpret those tacit notions and meanings, in the narrative itself, as well as the interaction between the narrator and interviewer.

When analyzing narratives, ethnographers draw on approaches similar to those that are involved in textual and literary analysis. These include efforts to discern and interpret the following:

- **Form and structure**. Every story has a sequence of events, and stories are also usually broken up into distinct periods. What is the sequence of action and what are those periods? What are the linkages the narrator makes between periods?
- **Contingencies**. All narratives highlight specific circumstances or idiosyncrasies that shape details and outcomes. These are often reflected in "critical junctures," where several viable things could occur (Neuman 2011). What are those contingencies and critical junctures?
- **Rhetorical devices**. Rhetorical devices and figures of speech such as metaphor, colloquialisms, irony, and similes often reveal symbolic ideas rooted in a conceptual order. What rhetorical devices does the

narrator use, and what might they reflect about the conceptual or symbolic order shaping the narrative?

- **Interactions**. Narratives are not simply about action and plot but also focus on interactions between individuals—including those who are within the narrative as well as between a narrator and interviewer. A focus on interactions within the story can highlight dynamics and contexts of social relationship in a community. A focus on interactions between interviewer and narrator can highlight contexts of storytelling, as well as how the story might change depending on whom it is being told to. What are those interactions between individuals in the narrative? What interactions between narrator and interviewer might affect the way the story is told?

12.3   An Exercise in Narrative Analysis

For this exercise, you need a story that has been spoken and then written down. It could be in your field notes; if so, it should be at least a few pages long. If you don't have one, direct yourself online to the narrative-driven radio program "This American Life" (http://www.thisamerican-life.org/), or the national oral-history project StoryCorps (https://story-corps.org/), both of which produce interviews around stories. Choose a story from one of these websites that interests you, and print out a transcript of it. With each successive pass through the story you are working with, jot notes here about the following:

1. Form and structure: _____

_____

_____

2. Contingencies: _____

_____

_____

3. Rhetorical devices: _____

_____

_____

4. Interactions: _____

_____

_____

DIRECTED LEARNING • ACCURACY AND ATTENTION TO DETAIL • CRITICAL THINKING

Reflection: Are there any patterns in the narrative that appear especially important and meaningful? How and why are they meaningful?

_____

_____

_____

_____

_____

_____

_____

_____

_____

_____

_____

_____

_____

_____

_____

_____

_____

_____

_____

_____

_____

_____

_____

_____

_____

_____

_____

If processing your field notes feels like it draws on techniques similar to those you might be using in a course on literary analysis, you're on the right track. In fact, there are various other techniques that literary scholars use to get at the meaning, style, and context of written documents that anthropologists can also employ in coding and analyzing their field notes. These techniques might involve close attention to imagery, symbolism, tone, character, etc., in the text, or the systematic application of particular theoretical perspectives to the text itself. But there are important differences between literary and ethnographic analyses. One of the most important is that as a fieldworker you have direct personal experience, head notes, intuitions, and various other data sources you're bringing to the subject that enable a level of nuance and contextualization not always available to literary scholars who don't produce the works they analyze. But this nuance and contextualization doesn't come easily, and there is yet another dimension of processing field notes to help you get there, and that is writing up your ethnographic account. We turn to this issue in the last chapter.

Space for Extra Notes

CHAPTER THIRTEEN

CRAFTING AN ETHNOGRAPHIC ACCOUNT

The transition from "fieldwork" to "deskwork" is most firmly felt when it comes time to craft an ethnographic account. The physical and (perhaps) emotional distance from the everyday relationships and experiences of the field has grown, and attention has fully shifted to considerations around how to write about the mixture of stories and ideas generated by fieldwork.

The work of writing an ethnographic account is never a matter of simply assembling and reporting "what is in the data" or explaining our understandings to others. Just as coding and analyzing field notes formulate understanding, writing is, in its own right, a process of sense making and continued learning. We clarify our thinking by doing it, and it is not uncommon for the thesis or argument to come into view only after the writing has begun, as theoretical insights are woven together with field note excerpts and stories. This process is a creative one, involving, as Clifford Geertz once observed, the crafting of "fictions[,] in the sense that they are 'something made,' 'something fashioned'—the original meaning of *fictio*—not that they are false, unfactual, or merely 'as if' thought experiments" (Geertz 1973: 15). Ethnographic writing is thus artful *and* truthful (Van Maanen 2011).

There is no formula for writing an ethnographic account. There are, however, a number of distinct literary genres of ethnographic writing, each with

> **KEY RESOURCE.** John Van Maanen's book *Tales of the Field: On Writing Ethnography* (Van Maanen 2011) has an engaging and accessible overview of the range of ethnographic genres. It also offers a useful entry point for exploring literary criticism about "writing culture"—the politics of anthropology as a form of literature—much of which happened in the 1980s and 1990s.

their own unique objectives and stylistic conventions. Three in particular, found in the table on the next page, are most likely to be of concern to undergraduates writing an ethnographic account.

Each genre carries its own opportunities and limitations. But these are ideal types, and any actual text probably diverges in various ways from these details, and some will actively blur the lines between genres. The important point is to recognize that *how* something is written—specifically an author's representational objectives and stylistic conventions—affects *what* readers will learn about it.

For most undergraduates, the ethnographic account will probably take shape as a term paper or be folded into a research proposal, with various formal expectations determined by the professor. Where these details are not predetermined, most ethnographic writers start by identifying potential models (journal articles, book chapters, essays) and aspiring in some fashion to incorporate or emulate their style and conventions. (There's a lot more to it than I'm letting on, involving a lot of reading—good *writers* are always *reading*—identification of the audience, willingness or desire to experiment with form, and other factors.)

Whatever those formalities are, however, keep in mind that readers of any ethnographic account will want to know:

- **The problem.** What is the problem under investigation, and what questions is the research seeking to answer?
- **The process.** Where, when, with whom, and how was fieldwork conducted?
- **The findings.** What did you learn about the problem from this research project?

As the writing begins, you are likely to have somewhat ready answers to the first two questions, while the findings—what you actually learned—are hazier. Coding, memos, and narrative analysis should have identified certain themes, of course. But now the goal is to clarify and render these themes into a

GENRE	SOCIAL REALISM	FIELDWORK NARRATIVE	CULTURAL ANALYSIS
Goal	To report and explain social reality	To communicate about existential and collective experience	To interpret symbolic meanings, analyze informal cultural logic, or describe "thickly"
Description of . . .	Behavior; social institutions, patterns, and structures; or material culture	Stories about the lived experiences of others and/or/with the ethnographer	Texts, symbols, narratives, meanings, cultural puzzles, or power relations
Analytical objectives	Explanation, theory building and testing	Narrative analysis; understanding of existential lifeworlds	Cultural interpretation, theorizing cultural processes, critique
Some theoretical approaches associated with genre	Positivism, empiricism, Marxism, functionalism, structuralism	Autoethnography, phenomenology, dialogical anthropology, intersubjectivity	Interpretive and symbolic anthropologies, postmodern social theory, postcolonial theory, queer theory, certain feminisms
Authorial voice	Omniscient authority, dispassionate and third-person voice	Personalized authority, often first-person voice	Willful author who utilizes dispassionate third-person or first-person voice; often navigates and manages discordant voices within text
Ethnographer's position in text	Concealed	Key character	Absent to present
Representative examples	Malinowski 1922, Evans-Pritchard 1940, Nash 1993, Rappaport 2000	Hayano 1982, Ellis 1995, Behar 1997, Poulos 2009	Geertz 1973, Rabinow 1977, Rosaldo 1989, Abu-Lughod 2000

(Table loosely adapted from Van Maanen 2011, Narayan 2012, and OSEA n.d.)

KEY RESOURCE. Kirin Narayan's book *Alive in the Writing: Crafting Ethnography in the Company of Chekhov* (Narayan 2012) is a rich wellspring of practical and profound perspectives—as well as guided writing activities—on the craft of ethnographic writing.

trustworthy narrative that is somehow credible, plausible, transferable, dependable, and confirmable (see chapter 1). Rather than provide any specific recipes about how to construct an ethnographic account—because there *is* no single recipe—the exercises below have you work through different elements that will play a role in crafting your ethnographic account.

Ethnographic Descriptions, "Thick" and Evocative

Crafting an ethnographic account involves descriptive writing about people, events, scenes, and action. These descriptions are more refined than anything in your field notes or memos, with more attention given to rewriting and editing them for flow and style. Done well, creating these descriptions can help you see dimensions of your subject you hadn't considered before. At the same time, they should be both convincing and evocative, setting scenes with vivid language and close description to transport readers to new imaginative spaces and intellectual revelations.

A key strategy for achieving these goals is what anthropologist Clifford Geertz called "thick description," borrowing a term originally used by philosopher Gilbert Ryle. For Geertz, thick description is less a set of specific techniques or procedures than a form of writing and analysis that "aid us in gaining access to the conceptual world in which our subjects live so that we can, in some extended sense of the term, converse with them" (Geertz 1973: 24). The goal of thick description is interpretation, "thick" enough that it, as Geertz said, "takes us into the heart of that of which it is the interpretation" (Geertz 1973: 18).

COMMUNICATION • CRITICAL THINKING

| **13.1** | **Approaching "Thick Description"** |

The full excerpt of what Geertz wrote is, "A good interpretation of anything—a poem, a person, a history, a ritual, an institution, a society—takes us into the heart of that of which it is the interpretation" (Geertz 1973: 18). The example he gave, again from Gilbert Ryle, was the thick description required to explain the difference between a wink and a twitch. To appreciate what he meant, you will create a "thick description," with no technical direction, keeping in mind his observation above. With a word processor write for about 20 minutes about a situation or phenomenon you encountered in your fieldwork. Print it up and attach it here.

To reflect: What makes your description "thick"? How does a description succeed, or fail, at getting "to the heart" of the issue or phenomenon you describe?

Of course, anthropologists don't (usually) describe the differences between winks and twitches. They describe people, their lives, events, and places. Getting to the "heart" of something so complex and dynamic is daunting. Keith Basso, an anthropologist known widely for the elegance and power of his descriptive writing about people and place, summarizes the challenge of ethnographic description in this way: "Heaven, then, in a few grains of carefully inspected sand; instructive statements about places and their role in human affairs through the close contextualization of a handful of telling events" (Basso 1996: 110). One of Basso's key strategies in crafting that "close contextualization" is to set down in writing evocative depictions of people, events, and especially places, such as this one, in which he writes about a horse ride he took with a Western Apache man during fieldwork:

> *August 10, 1982. But for a gate left carelessly open—and some thirty head of cattle that quickly passed through it to lose themselves in a tumbled maze of rock-strewn buttes, meandering arroyos, and dry box canyons—my instructional ride with Dudley Patterson might have proceeded as planned. The day began on a calm and peaceful note. We mounted our horses shortly after dawn, rode out of Cibecue on a trail leading north, and then turned east as the rising sun, a brilliant crimson ball, moved into view on a tree-covered ridge. The morning air was crisp and cool, and all one could hear was the comforting squeak of saddle leather and the hooves of the horses striking softly into the earth. A red-tailed hawk banked on the wind in a vast blue sky (Basso 1996: 141).*

Notice how he draws in the reader by setting a scene that helps you get a strong feeling for the landscape. Now you try.

13.2 Evoking Place

COMMUNICATION

Identify a meaningful place where you conducted fieldwork. It could be outside, like Basso's above, or inside somewhere. Write a five- to six-sentence paragraph describing that scene, using strong visual language, all your senses, and techniques such as metaphor to evoke the place for the reader.

_____

_____

_____

_____

_____

_____

_____

_____

_____

ACCURACY AND ATTENTION TO DETAIL

Of course, ethnographic accounts also produce descriptions of people who collaborate in the fieldwork. Although the ethical commitment to protect the identities of those collaborators typically leads ethnographic writers to anonymize people in their writing—primarily by changing their names and hiding any key identifiers that would enable the person to be singled out—this does not mean we shouldn't strive to write thick and evocative descriptions of the individuals we have observed and listened to closely during fieldwork. The goal is to get beyond a writing style that represents individuals as socially programmed actors, and instead to craft portraits of people that show them as characters with distinctive personalities, routines, and ways of being.

13.3　People Portraits

In her book *Alive in the Writing*, Kirin Narayan (Narayan 2012: 49–50) has a wonderful exercise that I've adapted here to help you begin preparing to write about a person, not as a socially programmed actor but a real, socially situated person with distinctive qualities of individuality. Choose someone central to your research whom you have observed closely (or a roommate or friend if you don't yet have such a person in mind) and jot down ideas about the following:

COMMUNICATION

- Unique physical feature(s):
- Distinctive quirk or mannerism:
- Something that gives the person delight:

- Preferred food or drink:
- What others might say about this person:
- Resemblance to somebody else:
- Objects the person is associated with:
- What the person is like in motion:
- How the person interacts with others:
- Social position:

Now, write a five- to six-sentence portrait of that individual. Observe his or her appearance, mannerisms, and social location in relation to the themes that your fieldwork focused on.

_____

_____

_____

_____

_____

_____

In spite of what some of your writing teachers may have taught you, it is not a crime to use the first-person "I" in formal social-scientific writing. Although not all ethnographic writers include themselves in the text, situating one's self and experience can provide an effective strategy for linking different moments in space and time, or for exploring steps in your thinking (Narayan 2012: 98). This strategy is especially typical of autoethnographic writing (see chapter 10), but even writers not working in that vein can employ personal ethnographic experience to set a scene, raise questions, or provoke some thought.

13.4   Putting Yourself in the Scene

This exercise is another adaptation of an exercise from Narayan's useful text (Narayan 2012: 98). Think of an important moment in your fieldwork and describe the scene. Describe your experience and thoughts as the scene unfolded. What general insights, memories, connections to texts, or questions were generated by this scene?

COMMUNICATION • ACCURACY AND ATTENTION TO DETAIL

For developing ethnographic writers, concerns of "voice"—providing the sense of a "communicating presence" behind the words (Narayan 2012: 85)—are often paramount. On one level, this concern applies to your own authorial voice. The goal is to cultivate a writing style that earns and keeps the reader's attention. It avoids recitations of events and people that feel, on the one hand, flat and mechanical, or on the other hand, gratuitous and unnecessary. In thinking about how to do this, identify a writer—it could be an anthropologist, journalist, or novelist—whose work you admire, and identify what techniques—turns of phrase, rhythm, and other stylistic techniques—help that individual hold and keep your attention.

On another level, concerns about voice also apply to how we incorporate into our writing the voices of those individuals who participate in our fieldwork. Those voices typically constitute crucial evidence for ethnographic claims-making, and ethnographic accounts are often sprinkled with long quotations and dialogues. Ethnographic writers work to become effective at identifying and protecting the uniqueness of those voices, which involve matters of editing and ethics, as we will see in the next two exercises.

COMMUNICATION • CRITICAL THINKING

13.5 Working with Other Voices

In moving from raw field notes to ethnographic account, it is usually necessary to edit raw notes of dialogue or what people told you in interviews to create a coherent quotation or excerpt to include in your text. Some of this work is somewhat mechanical, such as getting rid of "um" and other verbal placeholders and rendering oral statements into sentences with punctuation. But one also wants to protect key aspects of that voice, such as texture, cadence, and intonation. If you were a sensitive note taker, you jotted down notes about pitch, tone, etc., that can jog your memory. Identify a long, raw passage from a memorable interview you conducted, with someone whose spoken voice you found strong and captivating. With a word processor describe the key features of that voice. Now, edit/rewrite a section of the interview (aim for a passage of about 8–10 sentences), to render it into a quotation that might be useful in your text. Be careful to protect that person's voice.

Reflection: Do you think you protected that distinctive voice? How? Do you think you lost anything about it in editing it?

_____

_____

_____

_____

_____

COMMUNICATION • CRITICAL THINKING

13.6 Ethical Reasoning: Writing and Anthropological Responsibilities

Review the AAA Principles of Professional Responsibility through the lens of writing an ethnographic account. Are there any particular principles in that table that apply to writing ethnographic accounts specifically? What are they and how do they relate?

_____

_____

_____

_____

To whom are you responsible when you write an ethnographic account?

_____

_____

_____

_____

_____

What do you think it means to write an ethical ethnographic account?

_____

_____

_____

_____

_____

_____

These exercises barely scratch the surface of the many possibilities to strengthen your ethnographic account by paying closer attention not just to *what* you write but to *how* you write. You still have to pull it all together, though, by working out what the *what* is. The next exercise pushes you in that direction, the goal being to get you working through how to connect story with ideas, which is the impulse that lies at the heart of ethnographic communication.

13.7   Weaving Together Story and Ideas

<u>Part 1</u>. Write about an experience or a story derived from fieldwork connected to the theme your paper will focus on. If nothing jumps out at you, look for turning points, conflicts, hardships, beginnings, successes, or failures in your notes; in other words, situations of mundane, everyday drama (Narayan 2012). Describe closely and in detail what happened, as well as the setting, who was there, and the action. Keep it to one page.

DIRECTED LEARNING

COMMUNICATION • ACCURACY AND ATTENTION TO DETAIL • CRITICAL THINKING

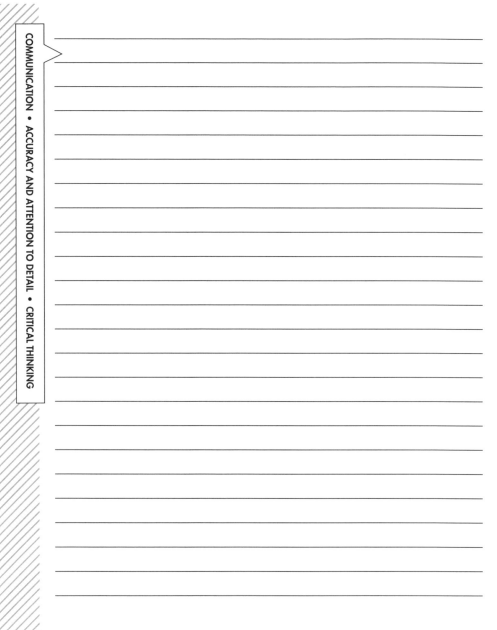

Part 2. Now write about why you think this situation is important. Here you should identify any "guiding ideas" (Narayan 2012) that brought your attention to this experience or story. You don't necessarily need to bring in formal theories here, but if you can identify any theoretical ideas that have special significance to this situation, see if you can explain, in simple language, what that significance is.

Much of what remains in ethnographic writing—and there *is* much that remains—involves variations on or scaling up the kind of work done in exercise 13.7. Sometimes it will be stories that drive your writing, and other times it will be ideas or theories. Whatever the case, story and idea are always likely to be intertwined in some shape or form because that effort is what defines the writing as *ethnographic*. Moreover, in addition to attentiveness to some of the stylistic elements introduced before, part of what will distinguish *your* writing voice as an anthropological author will lie in how you deliberately and thoughtfully weave those elements together. And if there's ever a time to say, "just go do it," perhaps now is it. Just go do it.

Space for Extra Notes

Acknowledgments

Writing this book has been a playful and creative experience. My profuse thanks to Meredith Keffer, an assistant editor with Oxford University Press (OUP), who posed the initial concept, and to Sherith Pankratz, executive editor, who always knows a great idea when she sees one and, more importantly, makes it happen. I am grateful to both for their editorial wisdom and enthusiastic support of this and my other OUP projects. At OUP, thanks are also due to art director Michele Laseau, project manager Christian Holdener, and copyeditor Tod Benedict. At the University of Vermont (UVM), I am fortunate to have some excellent colleagues in the Department of Anthropology who have aided, abetted, and enriched my various intellectual and pedagogical projects, including this one. Chief among these is Ben Eastman, who always has an encouraging word and insightful comment to share. In addition to sharing an excerpt from his own field notes here, he has aided this project by offering counsel drawn from his own deep wellspring of anthropological sophistication and pedagogical creativity. Jonah Steinberg and Teresa Mares have also supported this project generously with their own field note excerpts and wise counsel. I am also grateful to Rob Gordon, Rob Welsch, and Rena Lederman, who over the years have guided and shaped my thinking about fieldwork in various ways. I received valuable feedback from 10 reviewers, and this book is better in no small part because of their thoughtful and constructive reading. A draft of this book was "field tested" with 21 students in my spring 2016 Introduction to Cultural Anthropology class at UVM. They took on the job with gusto, and their experiences and recommendations helped refine many of its guided exercises. UVM seniors Leah Rogstad, Cara Zhuang, and Olivia Sorci also provided me with substantive suggestions for refinement. My wife, Peggy, and our kids, Isabel, Felipe, and Camila, as ever, indulge my play-making as an anthropologist and are, in important respects, fellow travelers in a life enriched by fieldwork. My sincere gratitude to them.

Manuscript Reviewers

I have greatly benefited from the perceptive comments and suggestions of the many talented scholars and instructors who reviewed the proposal for *Field Notes*.

Their insight and suggestions contributed immensely to the published work.

Keri Brondo, University of Memphis

Kimberly K. Cavanagh, University of South Carolina, Beaufort

Benjamin Eastman, University of Vermont

Ruth Gomberg-Muñoz, Loyola University Chicago

Kathe Managan, Louisiana State University

David McCaig, Phoenix College

Mark Moritz, Ohio State University

Laura M. Tilghman, Plymouth State University

Jennifer R. Wies, Eastern Kentucky University

One anonymous reviewer

Bibliography

Abu-Lughod, Lila. 1991. "Writing against Culture." In *Recapturing Anthropology: Working in the Present*. Edited by Richard G. Fox, 50–9. Santa Fe, NM: School of American Research Press.

Abu-Lughod, Lila. 2000. *Veiled Sentiments: Honor and Poetry in a Bedouin Society*. Updated ed. Berkeley: University of California Press.

Agar, Michael H. 1996. *The Professional Stranger: An Informal Introduction to Ethnography*. 2d ed. San Diego, CA: Academic Press.

Amit, Vered. 2000. "Introduction: Constructing the Field." In Vered Amit, ed. *Constructing the Field: Ethnographic Fieldwork in the Contemporary World*. Edited by Vered Amit, 1–18. London: Routledge.

Andrews, Hazel. 2012. "Mapping My Way: Map-Making and Analysis in Participant Observation." In *Mapping Cultures: Place, Practice, Performance*. Edited by Les Roberts, 216–36. New York: Palgrave Macmillan.

Banks, Marcus. 1995. "Visual Research Methods." *Social Research Update* 11 (Winter). Department of Sociology, University of Surrey, Guildford, UK. Available at http://sru.soc.surrey.ac.uk/SRU11/SRU11.html.

Banks, Marcus, and Howard Morphy, eds. 1997. *Rethinking Visual Anthropology*. New Haven, CT: Yale University Press.

Banks, Marcus, and David Zeitlyn. 2015. *Visual Methods in Social Research*. 2d ed. London: SAGE.

Basso, Keith H. 1996. *Wisdom Sits in Places: Landscape and Language among the Western Apache*. Albuquerque: University of New Mexico Press.

Behar, Ruth. 1997. *The Vulnerable Observer: Anthropology That Breaks Your Heart*. Boston: Beacon.

Berger, John, and Jean Mohr. 1982. *Another Way of Telling*. New York: Pantheon.

Boellstorff, Tom. 2008. *Coming of Age in Second Life: An Anthropologist Explores the Virtually Human*. Princeton, NJ: Princeton University Press.

Boellstorff, Tom, Bonnie Nardi, Celia Pearce, and T. L. Taylor. 2012. *Ethnography and Virtual Worlds: A Handbook of Method*. Princeton, NJ: Princeton University Press.

Chang, Heewon. 2008. *Autoethnography as Method*. Developing Qualitative Inquiry 1. Walnut Creek, CA: Left Coast.

Chapin, Mac, Zachary Lamb, and Bill Threlkeld. 2005. "Mapping Indigenous Lands." *Annual Review of Anthropology* 34:619–38.

Comaroff, John. 2010. "The End of Anthropology, Again: On the Future of an In/Discipline." *American Anthropologist* 112.4: 524–38.

Cooper, Becky. 2013. *Mapping Manhattan: A Love (and Sometimes Hate) Story in Maps by 75 New Yorkers.* New York: Harry N. Abrams.

Ellis, Carolyn. 1995. *Final Negotiations: A Story of Love, Loss, and Chronic Illness.* Health, Society, and Policy. Philadelphia: Temple University Press.

Ellis, Carolyn, Tony E. Adams, and Arthur P. Bochner. 2011. "Autoethnography: An Overview." *FQS Forum: Qualitative Social Research* 12.1: 10. Available at http://www.qualitative-research.net /index.php/fqs/article/view/1589/3095.

Ellis, Carolyn, and Arthur P. Bochner. 2000. "Autoethnography, Personal Narrative, Reflexivity: Researcher as Subject." In eds., Handbook of Qualitative Research. 2d ed. Edited by Norman K. Denzin and Yvonna S. Lincoln, 733–68). Thousand Oaks, CA: SAGE.

Emerson, Robert M., Rachel I. Fretz, and Linda L. Shaw. 1995. *Writing Ethnographic Fieldnotes.* Chicago Guides to Writing, Editing, and Publishing. Chicago: University of Chicago Press.

Emerson, Robert M., Rachel I. Fretz, and Linda L. Shaw. 2011. *Writing Ethnographic Fieldnotes.* 2d ed. Chicago Guides to Writing, Editing, and Publishing. Chicago: University of Chicago Press.

Evans-Pritchard, E. E. 1940. *The Nuer: A Description of the Modes of Livelihood and Political Institutions of a Nilotic People.* Oxford: Clarendon.

Fabian, Johannes. 1971. "On Professional Ethics and Epistemological Foundations." *Current Anthropology* 12.2: 230–2.

Feld, Steven. 1996. "Waterfalls of Song: An Acoustemology of Place Resounding in Bosavi, Papua New Guinea." In Feld, S. & Basso, K.H., eds. *Senses of Place.* Edited by Steven Feld and Keith H. Basso, 91–135. Santa Fe, NM: School of American Research Press.

Fluehr-Lobban, Carolyn, ed. 2003. *Ethics and the Profession of Anthropology: Dialogue for Ethically Conscious Practice.* 2d. ed. Walnut Creek, CA: AltaMira.

Geertz, Clifford. 1973. *The Interpretation of Cultures: Selected Essays.* New York: Basic Books.

Hammersley, Martyn, and Paul Atkinson. 1983. *Ethnography: Principles in Practice.* London: Routledge.

Hammersley, Martyn, and Paul Atkinson. 1995. *Ethnography: Principles in Practice.* 2d ed. London: Routledge.

Hayano, David M. 1982. *Poker Faces: The Life and Work of Professional Card Players.* Berkeley: University of California Press.

Horst, Heather A., and Daniel Miller, eds. 2012. *Digital Anthropology.* London: Berg.

Hovland, Ingie. 2007. "Fielding Emotions: Introduction." *Anthropology Matters* 9.1. Available at http:// www.anthropologymatters.com/index.php/anth_matters/article/view/51/98.

Ingold, Tim, ed. 2011. *Redrawing Anthropology: Materials, Movements, Lines.* Anthropological Studies of Creativity and Perception. Farnham, UK: Ashgate.

Kuznar, Lawrence A., and Oswald Werner. 2001. "Ethnographic Mapmaking: Part 1—Principles." *Field Methods* 13.2: 204–13.

LeCompte, Margaret D., and Jean J. Schensul. 1999. *Designing and Conducting Ethnographic Research*. Ethnographer's Toolkit 1. Lanham, MD: Altamira.

Malinowski, Bronislaw. 1922. *Argonauts of the Western Pacific: An Account of Native Enterprise and Adventure in the Archipelagoes of Melanesian New Guinea*. Studies in Economics and Political Science 65. London: Routledge & Kegan Paul.

Malinowski, Bronislaw. 1989. *A Diary in the Strict Sense of the Term*. Translated by Norbert Guterman. Stanford, CA: Stanford University Press.

Marcus, George E. 1980. "Rhetoric and the Ethnographic Genre in Anthropological

Research." *Current Anthropology* 21.4: 507–10.

McGee, R. Jon and Richard L. Warms. 2013. *Theory in Social and Cultural Anthropology: An Encyclopedia*. Los Angeles: Sage Publications.

McIntosh, Peggy. 1997. "White Privilege and Male Privilege: A Personal Account of Coming to See Correspondences through Work in Women's Studies." In *Critical White Studies: Looking behind the Mirror*. Edited by Richard Delgado and Jean Stefancic, 291–9. Philadelphia: Temple University Press.

Mead, Margaret, and Gregory Bateson. 2002. "On the Use of the Camera in Anthropology." In *The Anthropology of Media: A Reader*. Edited by Kelly Askew and Richard R. Wilk, 41–6. Blackwell Readers in Anthropology 2. Malden, MA: Blackwell.

Miller, Daniel. 2011. *Tales from Facebook*. Malden, MA: Polity.

Miller, Daniel, and Don Slater. 2000. *The Internet: An Ethnographic Approach*. Oxford: Berg.

Miner, Horace. 1956. "Body Ritual among the Nacirema." *American Anthropologist* 58.3: 503–7.

Narayan, Kirin. 2012. *Alive in the Writing: Crafting Ethnography in the Company of Chekhov*. Chicago: University of Chicago Press.

Nardi, Bonnie A. 2010. *My Life as a Night Elf Priest: An Anthropological Account of World of Warcraft*. Technologies of the Imagination. Ann Arbor: University of Michigan Press.

Nash, June. 1993. *We Eat the Mines and the Mines Eat Us: Dependency and Exploitation in Bolivian Tin Mines*. Rev. ed. New York: Columbia University Press.

Neuman, W. Lawrence. 2011. *Social Research Methods: Qualitative and Quantitative Approaches*. 7th ed. Boston: Allyn & Bacon.

OSEA (Open School of Ethnography and Anthropology). n.d. *OSEA Writing Ethnography Guidelines for Final Project Portfolio*. Available at http://www.osea-cite.org/resources/OSEA_Guide_to_Writing_Ethnography.doc.

Ottenberg, Simon. 1990. "Thirty Years of Fieldnotes: Changing Relationships to the Text." In *Fieldnotes: The Makings of Anthropology*. Edited by Roger Sanjek, 139–60. Ithaca, NY: Cornell University Press.

Pink, Sarah. 2013. *Doing Visual Ethnography*. 3d ed. Los Angeles: SAGE.

Pink, Sarah, Heather Horst, John Postill, Larissa Hjorth, Tania Lewis, and Jo Tacchi. 2015. *Digital Ethnography: Principles and Practice*. London: SAGE.

Postill, John, and Sarah Pink. 2012. "Social Media Ethnography: The Digital Researcher in a Messy Web." *Media International Australia, Incorporating Culture and Policy: Quarterly Journal of Media Research and Resources* 145 (November): 123–34.

Poulos, Christopher N. 2009. *Accidental Ethnography: An Inquiry into Family Secrecy*. Writing Lives—Ethnographic Narratives. Walnut Creek, CA: Left Coast.

Powdermaker, Hortense. 1966. *Stranger and Friend: The Way of an Anthropologist*. Norton Library N410. New York: W. W. Norton.

Rabinow, Paul. 1977. *Reflections on Fieldwork in Morocco*. Berkeley: University of California Press.

Rappaport, Roy A. 2000. *Pigs for the Ancestors: Ritual in the Ecology of a New Guinea People*. 2d ed. Long Grove, IL: Waveland.

Reed-Danahay, Deborah, ed. 1997. *Auto/Ethnography: Rewriting the Self and the Social*. Explorations in Anthropology. New York: Berg.

Robben, Antonius C. G. M., and Jeffrey A. Sluka, eds. 2012. *Ethnographic Fieldwork: An Anthropological Reader*. 2d ed. Blackwell Anthologies in Social and Cultural Anthropology. Malden, MA: Wiley-Blackwell.

Roberts, Les, ed. 2012. *Mapping Cultures: Place, Practice, Performance*. New York: Palgrave Macmillan.

Rosaldo, Renato. 1989. *Culture & Truth: The Remaking of Social Analysis*. Boston: Beacon.

Samuels, David W., Louise Meintjes, Ana Maria Ochoa, and Thomas Porcello. 2010. "Soundscapes: Toward a Sounded Anthropology." *Annual Review of Anthropology* 39:329–45.

Sanjek, Roger, ed. 1990. *Fieldnotes: The Makings of Anthropology*. Ithaca, NY: Cornell University Press.

Scott, Greg, and Roberta Garner. 2013. *Doing Qualitative Research: Designs, Methods, and Techniques*. Boston: Pearson.

Shenton, Andrew K. 2004. "Strategies for Ensuring Trustworthiness in Qualitative Research Projects." *Education for Information* 22.2: 63–75.

Spradley, James P. 1979. *The Ethnographic Interview*. New York: Holt, Rinehart and Winston.

Taussig, Michael. 2011. *I Swear I Saw This: Drawings in Fieldwork Notebooks, Namely My Own*. Chicago: University of Chicago Press.

Tuhiwai Smith, Linda. 2012. *Decolonizing Methodologies: Research and Indigenous Peoples*. 2d ed. London: Zed.

Turner, Victor W., and Edward M. Bruner, eds. 1986. *The Anthropology of Experience*. Urbana: University of Illinois Press.

Van Maanen, John. 2011. *Tales of the Field: On Writing Ethnography.* 2d ed. Chicago Guides to Writing, Editing, and Publishing. Chicago: University of Chicago Press.

Vivanco, Luis A. 2006. *Green Encounters: Shaping and Contesting Environmentalism in Rural Costa Rica.* Studies in Environmental Anthropology and Ethnobiology 3. New York: Berghahn.

Vivanco, Luis A. 2013. *Reconsidering the Bicycle: An Anthropological Perspective on a New (Old) Thing.* Routledge Series for Creative Teaching and Learning in Anthropology. New York: Routledge.

Wang, Tricia. 2012. "Writing Live Fieldnotes: Towards a More Open Ethnography." *Ethnography Matters* (August 2). Available at http://ethnographymatters.net/blog/2012/08/02/writing-live -fieldnotes-towards-a-more-open-ethnography/.

Werner, Oswald., and Lawrence A. Kuznar. 2001. "Ethnographic Mapmaking: Part 2—Practical Concerns and Triangulation." *Field Methods* 13.3: 291–6.

Winterbottom, Michael, dir. 2010. *The Trip.* New York: IFC Films.

Space for Extra Notes

Space for Extra Notes

Space for Extra Notes

Space for Extra Notes

Space for Extra Notes

Space for Extra Notes

Space for Extra Notes

Space for Extra Notes